CONTEMPORARY ENGLISH
BOOK 4

Elizabeth Minicz

Kathryn Powell

CB

CONTEMPORARY BOOKS

a division of NTC/CONTEMPORARY PUBLISHING GROUP
Lincolnwood, Illinois USA

Project Manager: Roseanne Mendoza
Cover Illustration: Regan Dunnick
Interior Illustrations: Regan Dunnick, David Rolfe, Jean Wisenbaugh

Acknowledgments

The authors and publisher would like to thank the following people for their help
and contribution to *Contemporary English:*
Series Consultant: **Catherine Porter,** Adult Learning Resource Center, Des Plaines, Illinois.
Reviewers: **Lisa Agao,** Resource Teacher, Fresno Adult School, Clovis, CA; **Bea Berrettini,**
Instructor, Fresno Adult School, Fresno, CA; **Lemuel S. Bonilla,** Professor, ESL, Santiago
Canyon College, Costa Mesa, CA; **Janice Bruno,** Instructor/Resource Teacher, Fresno Adult
School, Fresno, CA; **Mary Lou Byrne,** ESL Director, Triton College, River Grove, IL;
Clíf de Córdoba, Assistant Principal, Southgate Community Adult School, Los Angeles, CA;
Jill DeGrange, ESL Program Director, Salinas Adult School, Salinas, CA; **Samuela Eckstut,**
Senior Lecturer, CELOP, Boston University, Melrose, MA; **Stephen Ewert,** Instructor, Fresno
Adult School, Fresno, CA; **Eric Glicker,** Instructor, Rancho Santiago Community College District,
Santa Ana, CA; **Joyce Halenar,** Instructor/Advisor, Salinas Adult School, Salinas, CA; **Mary Jahr-
Purvis,** ESL Teacher, Salinas Adult School, Salinas, CA; **Robert Jenkins,** Assistant Professor,
Centennial Education Center, Santa Ana College, Santa Ana, CA; **Ruth Luman,** Instructor,
Long Beach Adult School, Long Beach, CA; **Sue Mendizza,** Coordinator, School of Continuing
Education, Santa Ana College, Santa Ana, CA; **Rachel Porcelli,** Independent Consultant, Dade
County, FL; **John Richardson,** Instructor, Fresno Adult School, Fresno, CA; **Judy Rosselli,**
VESL Instructor, San Diego Community College District, San Diego, CA; **Sandra Saldana,**
Lead Instructor, ESL Program, Triton College, River Grove, IL; **Kay Taggart,** Curriculum
Coordinator, Literacy and Workforce Development Center, El Paso Community College, El Paso,
TX; **Abigail H. Tom,** Instructor, Durham Technical Community College, Durham, NC.

Special thanks to **Jan Jarrell,** ESL Department Chair, Cesar Chavez Center, San Diego
Community College District, San Diego, CA, and **Donna Price Machado,** VESL Lab Coordinator,
San Diego Community College District, San Diego, CA.

Graphic and time line on page 10 from the book titled *Getting the Job You Really Want*
by J. Michael Farr. ©1995, JIST Works, Inc., Indianapolis, IN. Used with permission
of the publisher.

ISBN: 0-8092-0706-0

Project Manager: Roseanne Mendoza
Cover Illustration: Regan Dunnick
Interior Illustrations: Regan Dunnick, David Rolfe, Jean Wisenbaugh

Acknowledgments

The authors and publisher would like to thank the following people for their help
and contribution to *Contemporary English:*
Series Consultant: **Catherine Porter,** Adult Learning Resource Center, Des Plaines, Illinois.
Reviewers: **Lisa Agao,** Resource Teacher, Fresno Adult School, Clovis, CA; **Bea Berrettini,**
Instructor, Fresno Adult School, Fresno, CA; **Lemuel S. Bonilla,** Professor, ESL, Santiago
Canyon College, Costa Mesa, CA; **Janice Bruno,** Instructor/Resource Teacher, Fresno Adult
School, Fresno, CA; **Mary Lou Byrne,** ESL Director, Triton College, River Grove, IL;
Clíf de Córdoba, Assistant Principal, Southgate Community Adult School, Los Angeles, CA;
Jill DeGrange, ESL Program Director, Salinas Adult School, Salinas, CA; **Samuela Eckstut,**
Senior Lecturer, CELOP, Boston University, Melrose, MA; **Stephen Ewert,** Instructor, Fresno
Adult School, Fresno, CA; **Eric Glicker,** Instructor, Rancho Santiago Community College District,
Santa Ana, CA; **Joyce Halenar,** Instructor/Advisor, Salinas Adult School, Salinas, CA; **Mary Jahr-
Purvis,** ESL Teacher, Salinas Adult School, Salinas, CA; **Robert Jenkins,** Assistant Professor,
Centennial Education Center, Santa Ana College, Santa Ana, CA; **Ruth Luman,** Instructor,
Long Beach Adult School, Long Beach, CA; **Sue Mendizza,** Coordinator, School of Continuing
Education, Santa Ana College, Santa Ana, CA; **Rachel Porcelli,** Independent Consultant, Dade
County, FL; **John Richardson,** Instructor, Fresno Adult School, Fresno, CA; **Judy Rosselli,**
VESL Instructor, San Diego Community College District, San Diego, CA; **Sandra Saldana,**
Lead Instructor, ESL Program, Triton College, River Grove, IL; **Kay Taggart,** Curriculum
Coordinator, Literacy and Workforce Development Center, El Paso Community College, El Paso,
TX; **Abigail H. Tom,** Instructor, Durham Technical Community College, Durham, NC.

Special thanks to **Jan Jarrell,** ESL Department Chair, Cesar Chavez Center, San Diego
Community College District, San Diego, CA, and **Donna Price Machado,** VESL Lab Coordinator,
San Diego Community College District, San Diego, CA.

Graphic and time line on page 10 from the book titled *Getting the Job You Really Want*
by J. Michael Farr. ©1995, JIST Works, Inc., Indianapolis, IN. Used with permission
of the publisher.

ISBN: 0-8092-0706-0

CONTENTS

ABOUT THIS SERIES   iv

UNIT 1   **LOOKING FOR THE RIGHT JOB**   1
TOPIC: **Employment and Opportunity**

UNIT 2   **TRANSPORTATION UPS AND DOWNS**   13
TOPIC: **Transportation and Travel**

UNIT 3   **HELPING PEOPLE IN NEED**   25
TOPIC: **Home and Neighborhood**

UNIT 4   **ALTERNATIVE MEDICINE AND HEALTHY LIVING**   37
TOPIC: **Healthy Living**

UNIT 5   **CITIZENSHIP AND DOCUMENTATION FOR WORK**   49
TOPIC: **Employment and Opportunity**

UNIT 6   **ENTERTAINMENT AND THE ARTS**   61
TOPIC: **Arts and Entertainment**

UNIT 7   **OUR WATERS**   73
TOPIC: **History and Geography**

UNIT 8   **SAVING MONEY FOR THE FUTURE**   85
TOPIC: **Consumer Economics**

UNIT 9   **GETTING HELP IN YOUR COMMUNITY**   97
TOPIC: **Community Services**

UNIT 10   **MACHINES FOR COMMUNICATION**   109
TOPIC: **People and Machines**

APPENDIX   121

ABOUT THIS SERIES

PROGRAM COMPONENTS AND PHILOSOPHY

Contemporary English is a five-level interactive topic-based English-as-a-Second-Language series for adult learners ranging from the beginning-literacy level to the high-intermediate level. The series includes

- Student Books for classroom use

- Workbooks for independent use at home, in the classroom, or in a lab

- Audiocassettes for individual student, classroom, or lab use and

- Teacher's Manuals, with reproducible activity masters and unit progress checks for assessment.

These materials were correlated from inception to the California Model Standards for Adult ESL Programs, the MELT Student Performance Levels, and the SCANS (Secretary's Commission on Achieving Necessary Skills) Competencies.

Unique among adult ESL series, *Contemporary English* presents high-interest topics as a framework for developing a wide variety of language, thinking, and life skills. In addition to focusing on listening, speaking, reading, and writing skills, *Contemporary English* integrates work on language structures; problem-solving, critical-thinking, and graphic-literacy skills; and—increasingly important—work-related skills.

Contemporary English empowers students to take charge of their learning and to develop strong communication skills for the real world. For example, each unit in Books 1–4 falls under one of the following broad topics: Home and Neighborhood, People and Machines, Employment and Opportunity, Human Relations, Consumer Economics, Community Services, Transportation and Travel, Healthy Living, History and Geography, and Arts and Entertainment. (The lowest-level book, *Contemporary English* Literacy, addresses all of these topics except History and Geography and Arts and Entertainment.) In short, the series addresses topics of interest and concern to adult learners.

Contemporary English presents engaging and meaningful situations that provide a context for grammar structures, listening activities, and an emphasis on the world of work. Within this framework each unit offers a wealth of pair and group activities, often with designated team roles, and frequent individual and group presentations to the class. This approach mirrors the team organization characteristic of today's workplace and reflects the recent influence on education of the Department of Labor's SCANS report.

UNIT STRUCTURE OF THE STUDENT BOOKS

Contemporary English provides a controlled and predictable sequence of instruction and activities. Conveniently for teachers, each page of a unit functions as a self-contained mini-lesson. Each unit is divided into two parts, each of which begins with a **Scene** that presents, in comic-strip format, incidents from the lives of newcomers to the United States or aspects of U.S. culture that students encounter regularly. Lively, humorous, and dramatic, the **Scenes** engage students in the unit topics—usually by presenting typical problems in the lives of average people. A series of discussion ques-

tions proceeds from factual comprehension of the **Scene** to personalization and, in Books 3 and 4, problem solving.

After each opening **Scene** comes **Sound Bites,** a focused listening task that includes pre-listening and post-listening work. **Sound Bites** presents target content and language structures through lively conversations and other samples of natural speech, such as telephone answering-machine messages and transportation announcements.

Throughout *Contemporary English*, grammar structures are first contextualized in the **Scenes** and listening activities and then presented, practiced, and applied on follow-up **Spotlight** pages. Appearing two to four times in each unit, the **Spotlight** pages model target structures in contexts related to the unit topic. Special **Spotlight** feature boxes present the target structures schematically and provide brief, straightforward explanations when necessary. Exercises following the structure presentations allow students to manipulate the structures in meaningful contexts, such as stories or real-life situations. **Spotlight** pages usually end with a **Your Turn** and/or **In Your Experience** activity providing communicative application of the new structures.

These last two features, in addition to **Vocabulary Prompts,** occur within the units at the point of need, rather than in a fixed or unvarying part of each unit. **Vocabulary Prompts,** for example, serves to isolate challenging vocabulary before a listening or reading task. **Your Turn,** a follow-up to reading, listening, or structure practice, serves as a participatory task. **In Your Experience,** an activity drawing on students' prior knowledge and personal lives, allows learners to personalize the topics and relate them to their own experience.

Listening and speaking skills are developed further in the **Person to Person** activities, which present recorded two-person conversations exploring the unit topics in natural, colloquial language. Students listen to conversations, practice them, and work in pairs to complete a final open-ended dialogue. Students can then present their new conversations to the class.

Contemporary English helps students develop their reading skills and become motivated readers of English through **Reading for Real,** a page in each unit that provides stimulating authentic or adapted texts. With passages and realia that typically relate directly to the lives of characters in the **Scenes, Reading for Real** includes such real-life documents as a winning job résumé, instructions for office voice mail, biographies of real people, advice from the local police, and listings of music festivals around the country. Follow-up activities (such as **Your Turn** and **In Your Experience**) extend and personalize the reading.

Culture Corner provides further work on reading skills by focusing on the useful inside information about U.S. life that students love. Presented as brief readings typically paired with charts, graphics, or artwork, **Culture Corner** gives students the information they need to adapt to a culture that can often be confusing and difficult to understand. Interactive follow-up activities help students integrate cultural knowledge with their language skills.

Graphic literacy is the focus of **Get Graphic,** a feature that offers practice in reading charts, graphs, diagrams, and timelines—skills that are crucial in the workplace and for preparing for the GED. **Get Graphic** provides high-interest stimuli related to the unit topics and characters while it incorporates or recycles target language structures. A typical feature of this page is a follow-up activity in which learners develop their own simple graphs or charts and share them with partners or groups. The activities on this page help students learn to read, interpret, and use information in a graphic format.

Problem-solving and critical-thinking skills are developed further in **Issues and Answers.** This feature typically presents two opinions—often in direct opposition—in formats such as advice columns or letters to the editor. **Issues and Answers** contains short, humorous texts with views of U.S. life from a variety of perspectives, including those of immigrants and their "cultural advisors"—the experts who help to orient the newcomers as they bridge the gap between their native and adopted countries.

The last page of each unit contains a **Wrap-Up,** a project in which students use a graphic organizer such as a T-chart, a Venn diagram, an idea map, or a timeline to brainstorm and organize ideas and then talk or write in a group. Following **Wrap-Up** is the self-assessment activity **Think About Learning,** a final reflection task that asks students to evaluate the quality of their own learning on the major content points, life skills, and language structures in the unit. Students can thus assess what they have learned and provide feedback to the teacher, all of which helps to build a learner-centered classroom.

ABOUT BOOK 4

Book 4 focuses on high-interest topics such as the new workplace and the new skills it demands, consumer issues, and citizenship. Various ways for students to spend their leisure time are also covered, from the arts to volunteer work.

Throughout Book 4, learners are focusing on more complex language structures. The graphic literacy emphasis is particularly strong, in which students read, interpret, and create a variety of real-life graphs and tables. After completing *Contemporary English* Book 4, learners will be ready to move into any of several study or career paths, including pre-GED study, academic English as a second language, or workplace positions in which some degree of fluency is expected.

ICONS

Contemporary English uses the following six icons throughout the series:

 Listening—All conversations and other speech samples are recorded on tape.

 Speaking—Students speak with a partner, a group, or the class.

 Reading—Students read a passage, a graphic, or a short text.

 Writing—Students write letters, words, or phrases.

 Critical Thinking—Students perform an activity that requires critical-thinking skills.

 Spotlight—Students complete an exercise that provides practice on the structures presented on the **Spotlight** page. These exercises may require a variety of language skills, but structure practice is the principal focus of the exercise.

LOOKING FOR THE RIGHT JOB

Read the comic strip with a partner. Ask each other the questions below. Then share your answers with another pair or the class.

Pemba is talking to Susan at his neighbor's party.

FACTS	What's the problem? What are Pemba and Susan talking about?
FEELINGS	How does Pemba feel?
AND YOU?	Did you have a job in your native country? Do you have a different job in the United States? Which job do you like better?
COMPARISONS	Is it easier or harder to find a good job in the United States than it is in your native country? Explain.
ACTIONS	What should Pemba do? What do you think will happen next?

Now write or tell the story in your own words.

In small groups talk about the words below.

network   job lead   requirements   reference   apprenticeship

SOUND BITES

Listen to Pemba making some telephone calls to help find a job.

Before You Listen Read about the three calls that Pemba made.

While You Listen Write down the information Pemba got from each call.

1. Pemba called about getting a union card.

   How to get union card: *enroll in apprenticeship program.* _____

   Need: _____

2. Pemba networked (asked about job leads) by calling his friend, Nambi.

   Possible job: _____

   Where: _____

   Who to call: _____

   Best time to call for reference: _____

3. Pemba called 21st Century Construction to ask for an interview.

   Position: _____

   Requirements: _____

   Date and time of interview: _____

After You Listen With a partner compare your answers.

In Your Experience

Do a class survey about how people have gotten jobs.
Did they find out about jobs through friends, the newspaper,
or by going directly to businesses?
Write student names and responses in your notebook.

SPOTLIGHT ON PRESENT PERFECT

I've been a packer before.
He's driven a truck.

I haven't worked in a restaurant before.
She's never used kitchen equipment.

Have you worked in a factory before?
Have they ever worked in a restaurant?

Use the present perfect to talk about things that happened at some time in the past. The time is not specific, and the action may have happened once or many times.

Present perfect = *have* + (*not*) + past participle

Past — Now — Future

Regular verbs

I've operated factory equipment.
I've never used a cash register.
Have you ever trained other people?

Irregular verbs

I've done word processing.
I've never taken a typing class.
Have you ever gotten a promotion?

Exercise 1: Find someone in your class who has done the following things. Walk around asking questions, and have people answer and sign their names.

Have you ever . . .

worked in an office? _____   used a computer? _____

worked in a factory? _____   trained other people? _____

worked in a restaurant? _____   driven a truck? _____

been a cook? _____   had a job interview? _____

Exercise 2: Talk about your answers with a partner. For example, say, "(Isabel) has worked in an office."

In Your Experience

In your notebook draw a window like the one below and copy the words inside it. Then with a partner use the verbs from Exercise 1 to finish the sentences in the squares.

We have both . . .	I have . . . but my partner hasn't.
My partner has . . . but I haven't.	Neither of us has . . .

Person to Person

Listen to these conversations. With a partner finish the last conversation. Then practice the conversations with your partner.

1. Jay is asking Pemba about his background.

    JAY: Tell me about yourself.

    PEMBA: Well, I've worked as an electrician. I've also done factory work.

    JAY: How long did you work as an electrician?

    PEMBA: For two years.

    JAY: I see.

2. Jay is asking Pemba specific questions about his experience.

    JAY: What kind of work did you do as an electrician?

    PEMBA: I ran electrical wires in homes and businesses.

    JAY: Have you ever worked with computerized equipment?

    PEMBA: No, I haven't, but I'm a very fast learner.

3. Jay is asking Pemba about his strengths and weaknesses.

    JAY: What are your strengths?

    PEMBA: Excuse me?

    JAY: What do you do well?

    PEMBA: I'm very dependable, and I do good work.

    JAY: Do you have any weaknesses or things you need to improve?

    PEMBA: Well, I still need to improve my English. I've started taking a conversation class, and I'm learning a lot.

4. Jay is asking Pemba if he has any questions.

    JAY: You're from Nigeria? I'm curious. What religion are you?

    PEMBA: Is that important for the job?

    JAY: No, not really. Well, do you have any questions for me?

    PEMBA: Yes, I do.

> Employers should NOT ask you about your religion, age, ethnic origin, race, or marital status. It's illegal!

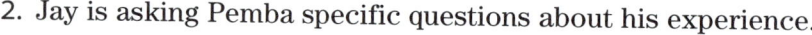

Your Turn

With a partner write a conversation with an employer. Write questions with "Have you ever . . . ?" Role-play your conversation for the class.

In small groups talk about the words below.

objective   qualifications   reliable   references available upon request

READING FOR REAL

Read Pemba's résumé and answer the questions below.

Pemba Ibo
1204 Cedar Drive, Apt. 3B
Charleston, SC 29410
(395)555-6294

OBJECTIVE   A position as an electrician

SUMMARY OF QUALIFICATIONS
Two years of experience as an electrician
Nine months of factory experience
Reliable and hardworking

EXPERIENCE
March 1998
to present   Assembler
                 Cinch Office Supply
                 3 Industrial Drive   Charleston, SC 29402
                 Promoted from packer to assembler
                 Drove a truck

1995–1997   Electrician
                 Porto Novo Electric Lagos, Nigeria
                 Did wiring in homes and businesses
                 Trained new employees

EDUCATION
May 1998 to present   English Classes, Charleston Adult School

1994   Electrician's Certificate
                 Lagos Technical Institute, Nigeria

REFERENCES   available upon request

1. What was Pemba's first job? _____*electrician*_____

2. What personal qualities does Pemba say he has? _____

3. How can Pemba's factory work help him get an electrician's job? _____

_____

Your Turn

With the help of a partner, write your own résumé. Look at Pemba's résumé as an example. Consider all your experience, even if you have not had a paid job before. Then ask another pair to read your résumés and help make corrections.

CULTURE CORNER

Read and answer the questionnaire. Then write answers to the questions below.

ARE YOU READY FOR THE JOBS OF THE FUTURE?

Jobs are becoming more and more complex. The U.S. Department of Labor talked to many employers to learn what skills are important for *all* jobs. The employers said that workers will need a *foundation*, or base, of certain skills and qualities. Are you ready for the jobs and society of the future? Circle *Yes, Sometimes,* or *No.*

A. Basic Skills:

Can you read and write well?	Yes	Sometimes	No
Are you good at mathematics?	Yes	Sometimes	No
Can you listen and speak well in English?	Yes	Sometimes	No

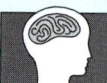

B. Thinking Skills:

Do you like to think of new ideas?	Yes	Sometimes	No
Can you make decisions?	Yes	Sometimes	No
Do you like to solve problems?	Yes	Sometimes	No
Can you understand graphs?	Yes	Sometimes	No
Are you a good learner?	Yes	Sometimes	No
Is it easy for you to see how things relate to each other?	Yes	Sometimes	No

C. Personal Qualities:

Are you responsible?	Yes	Sometimes	No
Do you feel good about yourself?	Yes	Sometimes	No
Do you get along well with others?	Yes	Sometimes	No
Do you know what you do well and what your goals are?	Yes	Sometimes	No
Are you an honest person?	Yes	Sometimes	No

1. Look at your *Yes* answers. In small groups discuss your strengths. For example, say, "I'm good at math. I can add numbers up quickly."

2. Look at your *Sometimes* and *No* answers. In your groups discuss some of the areas that you need to improve. For example, say, "It's difficult for me to speak English with strangers." Together, think of ways to learn and improve in these areas. For example, say, "You need to practice speaking more with your neighbors and your friends at work."

Read the comic strip with a partner. Ask each other the questions below.
Then share your answers with another pair or the class.

Pemba is talking with a job counselor at the adult school where his classes are.

FACTS	What's the problem? What is Pemba talking about?
FEELINGS	How does he feel?
AND YOU?	Have you ever felt the way Pemba does?
COMPARISONS	How do people find jobs in your native country?
	How is it different from looking for jobs in the United States?
ACTIONS	What do you think Pemba should do?
	What do you think will happen next?

VOCABULARY PROMPTS

Before you listen, talk about the words below in small groups.

concerns   outlet stores   candidates   reviews

SOUND BITES

While You Listen Take notes in your notebook. What concerns or questions does Jerry have? How does Pemba answer? Will he get the job? Explain.

SPOTLIGHT ON PRESENT PERFECT CONTINUOUS
WITH *FOR* AND *SINCE*

How long **have you been working** at the factory?

I've been working here for eight months.
I've been working here since March.

Use the present perfect continuous (*have + been +* present participle) to talk about experiences that started in the past and are still continuing. *For* describes a period of time (eight months, two years, five hours). *Since* describes a specific starting point (March 1980, 2:00 P.M.).

```
                      →
    ──────●──────────┼────────────────
    MARCH
          Past      Now       Future
```

You can use *for* and *since* with both the present perfect and the present perfect continuous.

Exercise 3: Pemba has written a letter to his friend Charles. Complete the letter with the present perfect continuous of the given verb, or *for* or *since*.

November 18

Dear Charles,

　　Sorry I haven't written (1) ___*since*___ June or July. I've really (2) *be*

_____ busy. How do you like California? We miss you at the factory.

　　I (3) *look* _____ for a job for the past few weeks. I've started

seeing a job counselor too. He (4) *help* _____ me write a résumé

and practice interviewing. This job change is very important to me.

　　I (5) *live* _____ in this country (6) _____ almost

a year, and it's time for me to get a better job. Send some news!

Your friend,
Pemba

Your Turn

Ask and answer questions with a partner. Use *for* or *since*. For example, ask, "How long have you been living in the United States? How long have you been working? How long have you been studying English?"

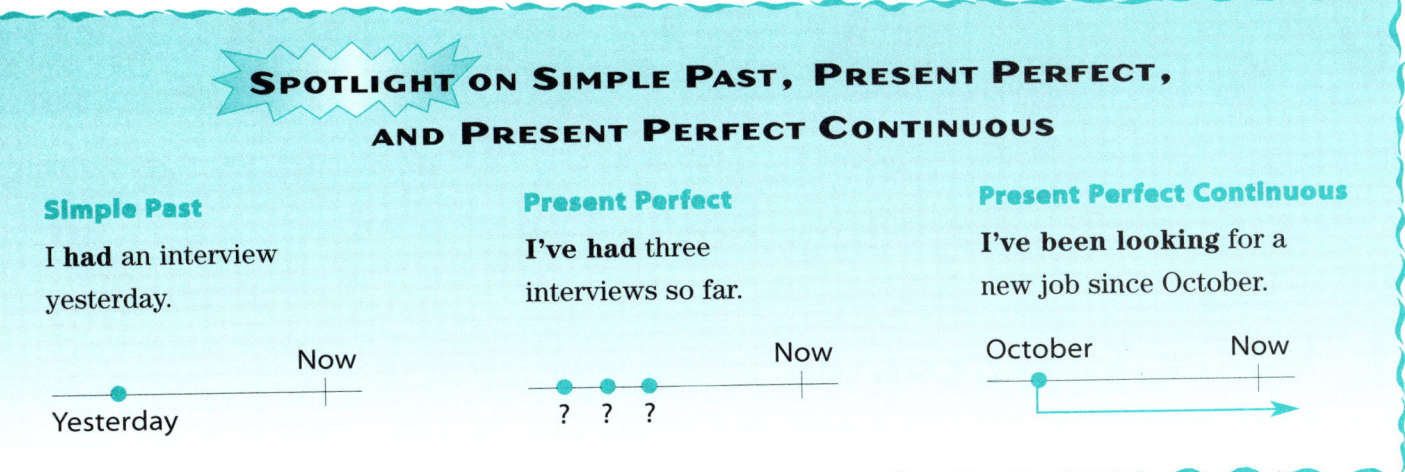

SPOTLIGHT ON SIMPLE PAST, PRESENT PERFECT, AND PRESENT PERFECT CONTINUOUS

Simple Past

I **had** an interview yesterday.

Present Perfect

I've **had** three interviews so far.

Present Perfect Continuous

I've **been looking** for a new job since October.

Exercise 4: Look at Pemba's calendar. Read the story and put each verb in the correct form: the simple past, the present perfect, or the present perfect continuous. There may more than one correct answer.

Jan.	Feb.	Mar.	Apr.	May	Jun.
moved to the United States		started working at factory			started studying English

Jul.	Aug.	Sept.	Oct.	Nov.	Dec.
		met Susan	called about union card		(now) applying at factory

Pemba (1) move ___*moved*___ to the United States in January. It is now December.

He (2) *live* _____ here for a year. He (3) *work* _____

at a factory since March. He (4) *start* _____ studying English in June.

He (5) *study* _____ English for seven months. Pemba (6) *meet*

_____ Susan in September. He (7) *know* _____ her for

three months. After meeting Susan, Pemba (8) *decide* _____ to work

as an electrician again. In October he (9) *call* _____ about getting a

union card. He (10) *decide* _____ to apply for a job as an electrician

at his own factory. He feels confident that he can learn the job.

Your Turn

Make your own calendar. Write down important things that have happened in your life in the past year. Then write a letter to a friend and talk about what has been happening in your life. Share your letter with a group or the class.

In small groups talk about the words below.

pie chart   job opening   want ad   competition

GET GRAPHIC

Study the time line and pie chart below.

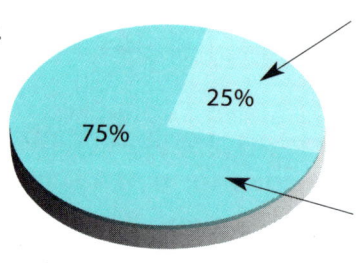

through wants ads, job listings, employment agencies

HOW PEOPLE FIND JOBS IN THE UNITED STATES

25%

75%

by talking to people and going directly to companies

THE HIDDEN JOB MARKET: HOW JOBS ARE REALLY FILLED

STAGE 1	STAGE 2	STAGE 3	STAGE 4
There is no job opening, but the company is always looking for good workers. Some lucky, qualified people apply and get jobs. Now 25 percent of all possible jobs are filled.	People *inside* the company know there is a new position. The "insiders" or their friends apply. At the end of this stage, 50 percent of all possible jobs are filled.	There is now an official job opening. People start hearing about it, and applications start coming in. At the end of this stage, 75 percent of all possible jobs are filled.	A "want ad" is put in the newspaper. Hundreds of people apply. At the end of this stage, jobs are 100 percent filled.

Exercise 5: In groups of two or three, write *true* or *false* next to the statements below.

1. The pie chart explains how to do well in an interview. _false_

2. More people get jobs by talking to people than by looking in the newspaper. _____

3. It's not a good idea to go directly to a company to ask about job openings. _____

4. In Stage 1 of the *Hidden Job Market*, it's impossible to get a job. _____

5. There is less competition for jobs in the early stages than in the later stages. _____

6. It is probably best to wait for Stage 4 to apply for a job. _____

In Your Experience

In groups talk about what you think is the best way to get a job. For example, say, "I think the best way to find a job is to talk to people you know."

Read the cover letter that Pemba wrote to send with his résumé.

December 15

Jerry Miller
Cinch Office Supply
3 Industrial Drive
Charleston, SC 29402

Dear Mr. Miller:

I am writing to apply for the position as an electrician.
I saw the opening in the November 26 <u>Company</u>
<u>News Bulletin</u>.

As you may know, I have been working at Cinch for
nine months. I also have two years of experience as
an electrician. I helped to hire and train new workers,
and I can work in different locations. I am very reliable and hardworking.

I recently got a promotion and a raise at Cinch, and I
would like to continue working here. I look forward to
discussing the position with you in person. I have enclosed
a résumé. Please contact me with any questions.

Sincerely,

Pemba Ibo

Your Turn

Find an ad for a job that interests you, either in the classified section of the newspaper or at your place of work. In your notebook write a cover letter to go with the résumé that you wrote for Your Turn on page 5. Have a partner read your cover letter and help you make corrections.

Date

Name of employer
Employer's address

Dear _____:

Paragraph 1: Write about the job you want. Tell how you heard about it.
Paragraph 2: Give a short summary of your experience and skills.
Paragraph 3: Say you are enclosing a résumé. Suggest a meeting.

Closing

WRAP-UP

In groups of three use the T-chart below to think of questions that an employer would ask you in an interview. Then work together to think of good answers.

QUESTIONS	ANSWERS

In the same groups of three, interview each other. (Two people ask the questions; the third person answers them.) Then talk about the interview. Were the answers clear or unclear? Was the person confident or nervous?

Think About Learning

In this unit you learned a variety of skills and language structures. Look at the items below and check how easy or difficult each one was for you. At the bottom write one other thing you learned.

SKILLS / STRUCTURES	Page	easy ☺	so-so 😐	difficult ☹
Talk about people's job problems	1			
Understand conversations about networking and getting references	2			
Read and write a résumé	5			
Do a career interest inventory	6			
Understand a time line	10			
Read and write a cover letter	11			
Think of possible interview questions	12			
Use present perfect tense	3			
Use present perfect continuous tense	8			

Read the comic strip with a partner. Ask each other the questions below. Then share your answers with another pair or the class.

Ted is at the airport, waiting for his wife's plane.

FACTS	Where are these people? What are they doing?
FEELINGS	How do they feel?
AND YOU?	Have you ever been in a situation like this?
COMPARISONS	Explain how meeting people at the airport is the same or different in your native country. Where do people meet their family and friends? What do they do when they meet them?
ACTIONS	What do you think will happen next?

Now write or tell the story in your own words.

VOCABULARY PROMPTS

Before you listen, talk about these words with the class.

clearance   deplane   destination   carry-ons   boarding call

SOUND BITES

Listen to the travel announcements Tessa heard on her recent trip.

While You Listen Fill in the chart below. Write the destination in column 2 and circle the special instructions in column 3. You can circle more than one answer.

Transportation	Destination	Special Instructions
1.		a. Get off the plane now. b. Remain seated until the seat belt sign has been turned off. c. Wait for the pilot to leave the plane.
2.		a. Sit in the front of the bus. b. Move to the back of the bus. c. Give your luggage to the driver.
3.		a. Give your ticket to the captain. b. Show your ticket to the steward. c. Leave the ferry for five minutes.
4.		a. Stay in the waiting lounge. b. Exit through the cashier's door. c. Pay the cashier.

After You Listen Work with a small group. Use the information in the chart to make one sentence about what people said in each announcement.
Share your sentences with another group. For example, say, "The flight attendant said, 'The plane from Miami has just landed.'"

Your Turn

Think of an announcement you heard recently. Try to write the announcement.
Read it to a partner. Ask the partner to guess where you heard this announcement.

SPOTLIGHT ON REPORTED SPEECH

Direct Speech

The flight attendant said, "The plane **has just landed**."

The captain said, "The ferry **will be leaving** in five minutes."

Reported Speech

The flight attendant **said that the plane had just landed**.

The captain **told us that the ferry would be leaving in five minutes**.

OR

The flight attendant **said the plane had just landed**.

The captain told us **the ferry would be leaving** in five minutes.

Pay attention to the verb tense change between direct and reported speech.

Example: Direct Speech: has landed   Reported Speech: had landed

                 Direct Speech: will be leaving   Reported Speech: would be leaving

The word *that* is often omitted in speaking and writing.

Exercise 1: In your notebook change these sentences from direct speech to reported speech. Use *that* in your first sentence. Omit *that* in your second sentence. Don't forget to change the verbs and the pronouns.

1. Raul said, "I need to get the brakes on my car fixed."

   Raul said that he needed to get the brakes on his car fixed.

   Raul said he needed to get the brakes on his car fixed.

2. Emma said, "I'm late to work because my car broke down."
3. Maria said, "I want someone to carpool to work with me."
4. John said, "I like to ride my bicycle to work on nice days."
5. Mel said, "I want to buy a new car next year."
6. Luke said, "I will be late for work tomorrow."

Your Turn

Think about three people you talked to today. What did they say?

Write three sentences using direct speech.

Then use reported speech to tell a partner what the people said.

For example, write, "My wife said, 'I have to work overtime tonight.' "

Then say, "My wife said she had to work overtime tonight."

Person to Person

Listen to these conversations. With a partner finish the last conversation.
Then practice the conversations with your partner.

LYNN: Hi. I'm renting a car this weekend, and I'm checking to make sure it will be a minivan.

CLERK: May I have your name and telephone number?

LYNN: Sure. It's Lynn Edwards, and my number is 325-555-6879.

CLERK: Just a minute while I check. Um, I have you down for a full-sized car.

LYNN: That's not right. The other agent said I could have a minivan.

ANNA: Some people at work were talking about taking a long weekend and going to the mountains.

CHARLES: That sounds like a great idea. But how much will it cost?

ANNA: They told me last year it cost about $300.

CHARLES: I'm not sure we can afford it.

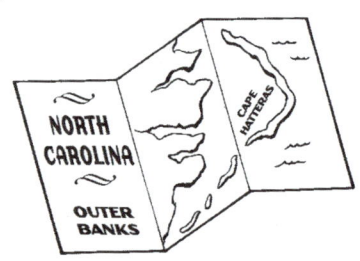

JOE: What are you looking at?

MARK: A travel brochure for the Outer Banks of North Carolina.

JOE: Are you going on vacation there this year?

MARK: I don't know yet. My wife told me she wanted me to surprise her, but I don't know if she means it!

KATE: Can I help you?

ROSE: My supervisor said you had forms for vacation requests here.

KATE: _____

_____

ROSE: _____

_____

In Your Experience

With a partner or a small group, talk about places you have traveled
to recently for work or vacation.

In small groups talk about the meaning of the words below.

awarded   service   in advance   subject to approval

READING FOR REAL

Before Ted takes a vacation, he needs to read his company's employee manual.

REQUESTS FOR VACATION

Paid vacation time is awarded according to years of service with the company.

1 year: 1 week	5–7 years: 3 weeks	11–15 years: 5 weeks
2–4 years: 2 weeks	8–10 years: 4 weeks	16 + years: 6 weeks

1. Requests for vacations of one or more weeks must be made one month in advance and are subject to the supervisor's approval.

2. Employees may take up to two weeks of vacation one day at a time. Requests for one-day vacations must be made no less than one week in advance and are subject to your supervisor's approval.

3. Requests for unpaid vacation are subject to your supervisor's approval.

Exercise 2: Use the information above to answer these questions about vacation requests.

1. Ted has worked at the company for two years. He has
   a. one week of paid vacation.
   b. two weeks of paid vacation.
   c. three weeks of paid vacation.

2. Who approves vacation requests at Ted's company?
   a. the owner
   b. other employees
   c. his supervisor

3. Can employees at Ted's company take unpaid vacations?
   a. no
   b. only one day at a time
   c. yes, with a supervisor's approval

4. How far in advance must week-long vacations be requested?
   a. a year
   b. a month
   c. two weeks

5. Ted wants to take one paid vacation day next week. Does his company allow this?
   a. yes, with a day's advance notice
   b. yes, with a week's notice and his supervisor's permission
   c. no, only with two weeks' notice

Talk About It

What is your company's vacation policy? Ask and answer for a relative or friend if you don't work. Why are vacations important for working people?

CULTURE CORNER

In many places in the United States, cars are necessary to get to work.
In most states teenagers get their driver's licenses at the age of 16,
but they usually start dreaming about owning a car long before that.
To many people having a car is as important as having a place to live.

In small groups survey each other about cars using the questions below.
Select a reporter from each group to share answers with the class.

- Do you have a driver's license?
- How old were you when you got your license?
- Do you own a car?
- When did you buy your first car?

- What kind of car do you drive now?
- What year is it?
- What is your dream car?

Exercise 3: In the United States many people do banking or eat in their cars.
In a group talk about the meaning of the words and the pictures below.

DRIVE-UP

DRIVE-THROUGH

Exercise 4: Write or talk about the answers to these questions.
Which of the two places in the pictures above have you been to?
Which ones do you think are useful? Why?

Your Turn

In a group make a list of *drive-ups* and *drive-throughs* in your neighborhood
or city. Then list some new ideas your group has for *drive-ups* and
drive-throughs. Share your two lists with another group or the class.

In Your Experience

Think about the question below. Write or talk about it with the class.
In your notebook, make a T-chart. Label one column *Advantages* and the
other column *Disadvantages*. Write the class's ideas in the columns. What
are the advantages of drive-up and drive-through places in the United States?

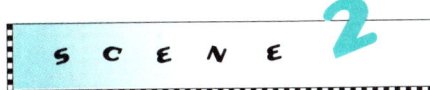

S C E N E 2

Read the comic strip with a partner. Ask each other the questions below.
Then share your answers with another pair or the class.

Ted and his wife, Tessa, are driving from the airport to the restaurant.

FACTS	What's the problem? What happened to Ted and Tessa?
FEELINGS	How do they feel?
AND YOU?	Have you ever been in a car accident? What happened?
COMPARISONS	What happens when people have car accidents in your native country?
ACTIONS	What do you think will happen next?

SOUND BITES

Ted is talking to his insurance agent, Craig Anderson.

Before You Listen In a small group talk about car insurance.
Ask the questions below. Share the information with the class.

Do you have a car?   How much are your premiums?
Do you have car insurance?   What is your deductible?

While You Listen Listen for the answers to the questions. Take notes.
What questions does the insurance agent ask Ted?
What does Ted have to fax to the insurance agent?

After You Listen Talk about the answers to the questions above.
With a partner write a conversation about an accident. Share it with the class.

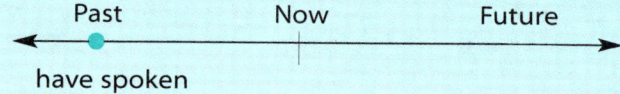

SPOTLIGHT ON PRESENT PERFECT

Ted **has** never **had** an accident before.

Ted **has** never **been** in an accident before.

Has Ted ever **had** an accident before?   No, he **hasn't**.

I **have** just **spoken** to my insurance agent.

Have you **spoken** to your insurance agent?   Yes, I **have**.

I've **gone** to the police station to pick up the accident report.

Have you **gone** to the police station yet?   No, I **haven't**.

```
        Past          Now          Future
    <---------●---------|---------------->
    have spoken
```

Use the present perfect (*have* + past participle) to talk about events and experiences at nonspecific times before the present time.

You can use the short forms *Yes, I have* or *No, I haven't* to answer questions with the present perfect.

Regular Verbs

Present	Past Participle
fax	faxed
arrange	arranged
call	called

Irregular Verbs

Present	Past Participle
find	found
hear	heard
send	sent

Exercise 5: Complete the conversations below.
Use the verbs and short answers above.

1. TESSA: Have you _____ that report to the insurance company?

   TED: No, _____.

2. TESSA: Have you _____ for a rental car yet?

   TED: Yes, _____.

3. TED: Has the repair shop _____ about our car yet?

   TESSA: No, _____.

4. TED: Has the insurance company _____ a check for the car rental?

   TESSA: No, _____.

Your Turn

With a partner use five of the verbs above or in the Appendix on page 121 to write your own conversations about car insurance or car repairs.
Share them with the class.

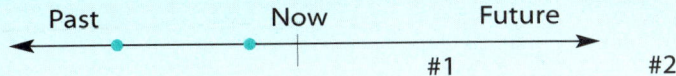

SPOTLIGHT ON PAST PERFECT

Event 1   **Event 2**

Ted and Tessa **had planned** to take a vacation before they had the car accident.

Event 1   **Event 2**

They both **had requested** three weeks off work before they had the accident.

<--------- Past ----------- Now ----------- Future --------->
                                              #1   #2

Use the past perfect (*had* + past participle) when one event in the past
happened before another event in the past.

Exercise 6: Read Ted's story. Write the simple past or the past perfect
form of the verbs in parentheses.

Ted (1) *work* __worked__ at Abcor Company for two years before he

(2) *take* _____ a vacation. He (3) *earn* _____ only two

weeks of paid vacation, but he (4) *decide* _____ to take a third week

of unpaid time. Tessa (5) *earn* _____ three weeks of paid vacation

time from her company.

Unfortunately, Ted and Tessa (6) *have* _____ a car accident a week

before their vacation. Ted (7) *stop* _____ at a red light when a car

(8) *hit* _____ him from behind. Tessa (9) *be* _____

so shocked that she couldn't stop crying.

Ted and Tessa (10) *decide* _____ to take their vacation anyway since

they (11) *request* _____ time off work. They (12) *plan* _____

to drive to the north woods of Wisconsin.

Your Turn

Tell a partner your own story about a time when you had had special plans
and something unexpected happened. Use the past perfect if you can.

GET GRAPHIC

Look at the map below. It shows the cost of round-trip air fares on 21st Century Airlines from Chicago, Illinois, to eight other cities in the United States.

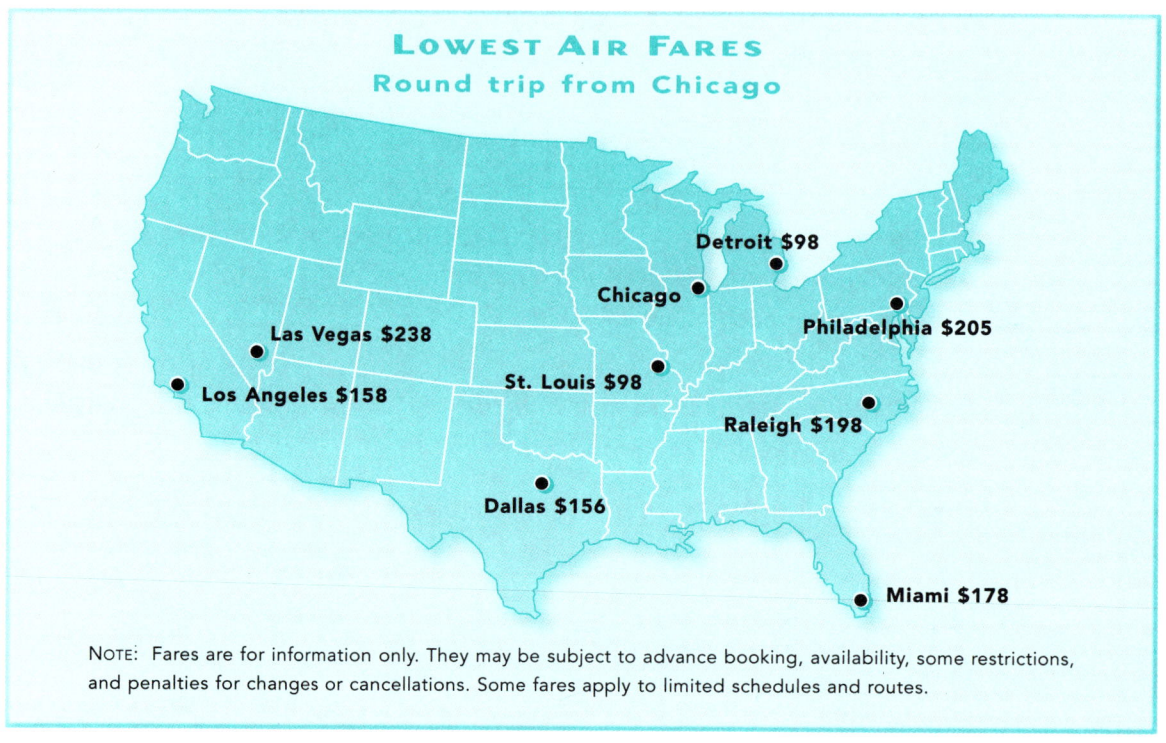

LOWEST AIR FARES
Round trip from Chicago

Detroit $98
Chicago
Philadelphia $205
Las Vegas $238
Los Angeles $158
St. Louis $98
Raleigh $198
Dallas $156
Miami $178

NOTE: Fares are for information only. They may be subject to advance booking, availability, some restrictions, and penalties for changes or cancellations. Some fares apply to limited schedules and routes.

 Exercise 7: In pairs, match the words in Column A with the words in Column B.

COLUMN A	COLUMN B
1. fare _____	a. reservation
2. dropped _____	b. ways to get from one place to another
3. booking _____	c. lowered
4. restrictions _____	d. limitations
5. routes _____	e. price

Exercise 8: Look at the map of 21st Century Airlines air fares again. Complete the sentences.

1. The cost of a round-trip ticket from Chicago to Los Angeles is _____.

2. The cost of a round-trip ticket from Chicago to Miami is _____.

3. The cheapest places to fly to and from Chicago are _____ and _____.

4. The most expensive ticket from Chicago is to _____.

5. Does this airline fly to Seattle? _____

ISSUES AND ANSWERS

Read the letters below. If you don't know the meaning of a word, use a dictionary or ask your teacher. Then write an answer to "Grieving."

Ask ABDUL and ANITA

DEAR ABDUL:

My wife and I were driving to a restaurant when we had a car accident. Fortunately, nobody was injured. The problem is that now my wife doesn't want to drive anymore. She is a nervous wreck in a car, and I don't know what to do about it.

TED

DEAR TED:

I think you need to give your wife some time to get over the accident. It is normal to be afraid after an accident. If she is still afraid in a month or two, ask her to see a counselor. Give her some time if you really love her.

ABDUL

DEAR ANITA:

My company gives employees two weeks of paid vacation time and five sick days a year. My favorite aunt died recently in another city. I asked my supervisor for time off for the funeral. He said that I had to take sick days or vacation days. I'm very angry, and I'm thinking about quitting. Don't companies have to give people time off to go to funerals?

GRIEVING

DEAR GRIEVING:

_____

_____

_____

_____

_____

_____

Exercise 9: Now write your own letter in your notebook, asking for advice about time-off problems or travel problems. Your partner will answer the letter.

Exercise 10: Present your letter and answer to the class.

WRAP-UP

With a partner ask and answer the questions below. Try to write three to five things in each box. Use reported speech to tell the class about your answers.

What are some things that both partners did in your native countries before you came to the United States?	What are some things that you did but your partner had not done?
What are some things your partner did but you had not done?	What are some things that neither of you had done before you came to the United States?

Think About Learning

In this unit you learned a variety of skills and language structures. Look at the items below and check how easy or difficult each one was for you. At the bottom write one other thing you learned.

SKILLS / STRUCTURES	Page	easy ☺	so-so 😐	difficult ☹
Talk about travel	13			
Understand travel announcements	14			
Read an employee manual	17			
Talk about things we do in our cars, such as eat or bank	18			
Understand a conversation with an insurance agent	19			
Read about air fares	22			
Read and solve problems	23			
Use a window to organize ideas	24			
Use reported speech	15			
Use the present perfect	20			
Use the past perfect	21			

HELPING PEOPLE IN NEED

Read the comic strip with a partner. Ask each other the questions below. Then share your answers with another pair or the class.

Neighbors are working to protect their city from a flood.

FACTS	What's the problem? What happened to these people?
FEELINGS	How do they feel?
AND YOU?	Has this ever happened to you? Has this ever happened to anyone you know?
COMPARISONS	Are floods a problem in your native country? What do people do when there are floods?
ACTIONS	What should these people do next?

Now write or tell the story in your own words.

Before you listen, talk about the words below in a group.

volunteer   shelter   lava   hurricanes   tornadoes

SOUND BITES

Gloria is a Red Cross volunteer. She is talking to her friend Juana.

While You Listen Number the pictures as Gloria talks.
What does she talk about first, second, third, and so on?

a. _____

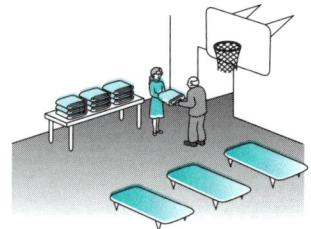

b. _____

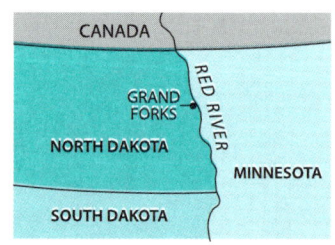

c. _____

d. _____

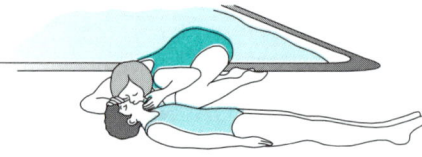

e. _____

After You Listen Use the numbered pictures to tell a partner Gloria's story.
Tell about the pictures in the same order Gloria talked about them.

Your Turn

Make a list of things you know about the Red Cross.
Read your list to a group or the class.

SPOTLIGHT ON THE PASSIVE VOICE

Active

A volcano **destroyed** my village.

A hurricane **hit** the East Coast.

The Red Cross **needs** volunteers.

Passive

My village **was destroyed** by a volcano.

The East Coast **was hit** by a hurricane.

Volunteers **are needed** by the Red Cross.

Use a form of *be* and the past participle of the verb to form the passive voice.

The phrase with *by*, sometimes called the agent, does not always appear.

Exercise 1: Read the sentences below about the Red Cross. Underline the verbs. Decide if the verbs in the sentences are active (A) or passive (P). Write *A* or *P* on the lines.

1. _____ The Red Cross helps people all over the world in times of war and peace.

2. _____ The Red Cross was founded in 1863 by Jean Henri Dunant from Switzerland.

3. _____ Dunant visited a battlefield in Italy in 1859.

4. _____ He didn't see anyone helping the wounded soldiers.

5. _____ Dunant wanted to help people, so he started the Red Cross.

6. _____ The United States did not join the Red Cross until 1881.

7. _____ Clara Barton, a nurse from Massachusetts, was chosen as the first president of the American Red Cross.

8. _____ Barton was known for helping the sick and wounded soldiers during the American Civil War.

Your Turn

In your notebook rewrite the sentences with active verbs. Make the verbs passive. Share your sentences with a partner or a group.

In Your Experience

With a group make a list of other helping organizations you know about. Share the list with the class. Have you or anyone you know ever been helped by the Red Cross or another group? Tell a partner or a group. Use the passive voice if you can.

Person to Person

Listen to these conversations. With a partner finish the last conversation.
Use passive voice verbs if you can. Then practice the conversations
with your partner.

MIGUEL: Are you going to the training session
tomorrow for the new cash registers?

TOMAS: No. I went last Tuesday.

MIGUEL: Is it hard to learn?

TOMAS: Not really. The directions are written
in simple English and Spanish.

AMI: What's that?

NIMA: It's a letter from a local charity.

AMI: Huh?

NIMA: I received it because I give to that
organization. Money is deducted from
my paycheck twice a month.

AMI: Why?

NIMA: They give money to help people in my
community.

MRS. TAN: What a beautiful vest!
Where did you get it?

MRS. SHAH: I bought it at the International Fair at
the Community Center.

MRS. TAN: Who made it?

MRS. SHAH: It was made by a Guatemalan woman
in one of the English classes.

BORIS: What's for dinner tonight?

SYLVIA: We have two kinds of soup and
a beef stew.

BORIS: Who brought all that?

SYLVIA: _____

_____

Your Turn

With a partner write a conversation using the passive voice about something you
heard or saw on the news recently. For example, write, "Hundreds of people were
laid off last week." Share your conversation with a group or the class.

VOCABULARY PROMPTS

In small groups talk about the meaning of the words below.

faulty   donation   household goods   generosity

READING FOR REAL

Read the memo from Human Resources and the thank-you note
Gloria received at work.

TO: All Employees of Flash Cable
FROM: Human Resources
RE: Fire at Susanna Mazur's home
DATE: July 25

Last night the home of Susanna Mazur
was destroyed by fire. Fortunately,
no one in the family was injured.
Fire department officials believe the
fire was started by a faulty water
heater. The family lost everything,
and they are currently staying in
a hotel. If you would like to make
a donation to the family, see Emily
in Human Resources.

Dear friends and co-workers:

My family and I sincerely thank you
for your kindness and generosity
after the fire at our home. Your gifts
of money, clothing, furniture,
and other household goods are
appreciated more than we can say.
I am very proud to work with such
wonderful people!

Sincerely,

Susanna Mazur and family

Exercise 2:   What happened when? Put the events reported above in order.
Number the sentences below from 1 to 6. Underline the passive verbs.
Then share your sentences with a group.

_____ A fire was started by a faulty water heater.

_____ Donations were received by the family.

_____ A home was destroyed by a fire.

_____ A thank-you note was sent to employees.

_____ Money, clothing, household goods, and furniture were given to the family.

_____ The Flash Cable Company was notified about the fire.

Talk About It

Talk about the questions below in a small group.

Have you ever been in a fire? What happened?

Has anyone you know ever been in a fire? What happened?

Would you donate anything to the Mazur family? Why or why not?

Do you think your company would ask employees to help each other?

Why or why not?

CULTURE CORNER

In a group talk about the volunteer activities in the chart.
If you need help, ask your teacher.

VOLUNTEER ACTIVITIES

Volunteer Activity	I have helped with this activity in the United States.	I have helped with this activity in my native country.	I am interested in this activity.
Lead Girl Scouts or Boy Scouts			
Feed the hungry			
Donate blood			
Visit senior citizens' centers			
Teach religious education			
Coach youth sports			
Work at immigrant aid associations			
Help out at children's schools			
Other:			
Other:			

Exercise 3: There are many different ways for people to help one another. Think about the volunteer activities in the chart above. Complete the chart by putting check marks in the columns.

Your Turn

In a group talk about the chart and your answers. Which volunteer activities were most people interested in? Which volunteer activities didn't interest many people? Choose a reporter and share the information with the rest of the class.

In Your Experience

Think about volunteer activities you have done. Complete the chart below and share it with the class.

VOLUNTEER ACTIVITY	WHERE I DID IT	WHEN I DID IT

Read the comic strip with a partner. Ask each other the questions below.
Then share your answers with another pair or the class.

Gloria's aunt, Luz Elena, lives in the Midwest, in Illinois.
Last week there was a tornado in her town.

FACTS	What's the problem? What happened to the house?
FEELINGS	How does Luz Elena feel?
AND YOU?	Have you ever seen a tornado or any other natural disaster? Where were you?
COMPARISONS	What natural disasters happen in your native country? What do people do after a natural disaster?
ACTIONS	What would you do if you were Luz Elena? What would you do if you saw a tornado coming?

SOUND BITES

Listen to the news reports on the radio.

While You Listen Fill in the chart below as you listen to the news.

WHAT HAPPENED?	WHERE DID IT HAPPEN?
1.	
2.	
3.	
4.	

After You Listen Check your chart with a partner, a group, or the class.
Use a map to locate the places mentioned in the news.

SPOTLIGHT ON PRESENT CONDITIONAL

Condition

If you live in the Midwest,
If there is too much rain,

Result

you can expect tornadoes.
rivers flood.

OR

Result

You can expect tornadoes
Rivers flood

Condition

if you live in the Midwest.
if there is too much rain.

Inference

You don't have to worry about tidal waves
You must be a caring person

Condition

if you live in Illinois.
if you are a Red Cross volunteer.

Use the present conditional to talk about things that are true or possible.
The most common way to begin a conditional clause is with the word *if*.
Use the present tense in the *if* clause.
Example: If you live in the Midwest, . . .

Exercise 4: Match Column A with Column B. Write the answers or say the sentences with a partner.

COLUMN A

1. If it doesn't rain for a long time, _____

2. Don't live near a river _____

3. If you want to help others, _____

4. People starve _____

5. People can go to shelters _____

COLUMN B

a. you can volunteer time or money.

b. if they don't have enough food to eat.

c. there is a drought.

d. if they have no place to live.

e. if you worry about floods.

Person to Person

Listen to the conversations. Practice them with a partner.
Then change them to be true for you.

MARY: I'm bored. I want to do something.

JOHN: I have plenty of things to do.

MARY: You always say that.

JOHN: If you're always bored, you must have too much free time. Why don't you volunteer someplace?

ERIC: You look really upset. What's wrong?

BILL: I had an argument with my boss today, and I can't stop thinking about it.

ERIC: You must really regret it if you can't stop thinking about it.

BILL: Yes, I should apologize to him tomorrow.

SPOTLIGHT ON CONDITIONAL WITH *WOULD*

Unlikely or Untrue Conditions

If I needed a place to stay,

If everyone had health insurance,

Results

I would call the Red Cross.

they would live longer.

Results

I would give more money to charities

We would end wars

Unlikely or Untrue Conditions

if I earned more money.

if there were no weapons.

Use the conditional with *would* to talk about things that are not true
or not possible.

Exercise 5: Complete the sentences. Then share them with a group.

1. If I had more time, I would _____.

2. I would _____ if I earned more money.

3. I would _____ if I had more education.

4. If I spoke better English, I _____.

5. If I had _____,

   I'd _____.

Your Turn

Read the facts about Alberto and Emma. Use the facts to write sentences.
Use the conditional with *would*. For example, write,
"If Alberto saved a lot of money, he would retire at age 50."
Share your sentences with a group or the class.

Facts about Alberto

1. saves a lot of money
2. always exercises
3. is always on time to work

Facts about Emma

1. drives carefully
2. never argues with anyone
3. wins the lottery

In Your Experience

Make a list of facts that are unlikely or untrue about your personal life,
work life, the United States, your native country, or the world.
Use the facts to write five sentences using the conditional with *would*
to share with the class. For example, write, "If I became president,
I would end unemployment."

GET GRAPHIC

Gloria's cousin Carmen lives in a suburb of Chicago, Illinois. Last week there was a tornado in Carmen's town. Many volunteers were needed to help clean up after the tornado.

Illinois had 307 tornadoes from 1990 to 1996. There were 31 deaths, but 29 of them were caused by one tornado in 1990.

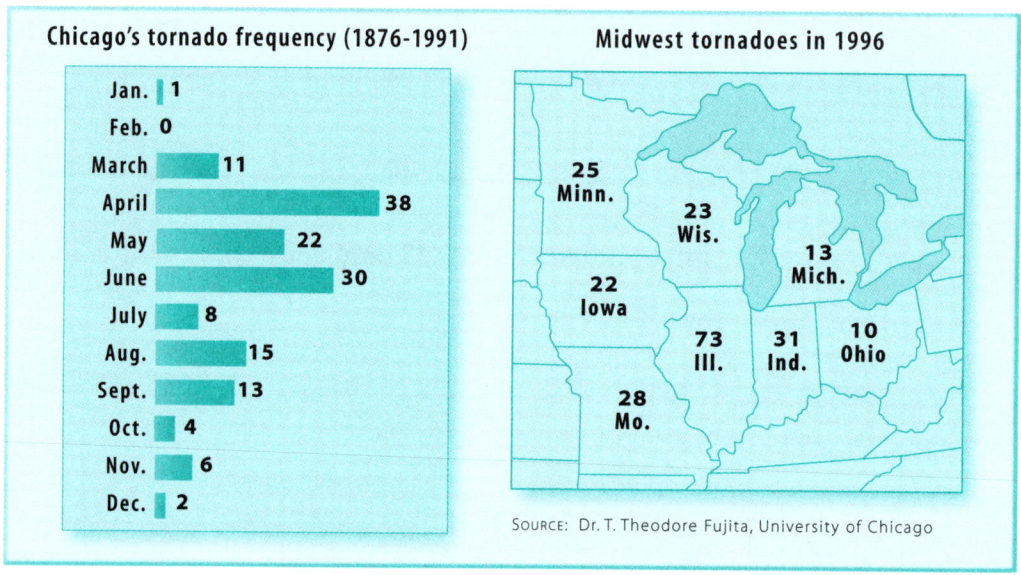

Chicago's tornado frequency (1876-1991)

Month	Count
Jan.	1
Feb.	0
March	11
April	38
May	22
June	30
July	8
Aug.	15
Sept.	13
Oct.	4
Nov.	6
Dec.	2

Midwest tornadoes in 1996

25 Minn.
23 Wis.
13 Mich.
22 Iowa
73 Ill.
31 Ind.
10 Ohio
28 Mo.

SOURCE: Dr. T. Theodore Fujita, University of Chicago

Exercise 6: Use the bar graph and the map to complete the sentences.

1. In the Midwest the state with the greatest number of tornadoes

   in 1996 was _____ .

2. The state with the smallest number of tornadoes was _____ .

3. Most tornadoes happen during the months of _____ ,

   _____ , and _____ .

4. The only month that has never had a tornado is _____ .

5. If you are worried about tornadoes in Chicago, the safest months

   of the year are _____ .

Brain Teaser: One reason there might be so many tornadoes

in the spring is that _____ .

In Your Experience

Do a survey. Ask questions such as, "How many people have been in a tornado? How many have been in a hurricane? How many have been in an earthquake? How many have been in a flood?" Use the answers to make a graph.

ISSUES AND ANSWERS

Read the letters to the editor below from a newspaper. If you don't know the meaning of a word, use a dictionary or ask your teacher.

FOREST HILLS—Poland recently experienced the worst flooding in two hundred years. One quarter of the country is under water. Over 140 cities are completely flooded. Two hundred thousand families had to leave their homes. Many regions have no food, water, or electricity. The flooding started three weeks ago, but your newspaper had only two small stories about it. I think that is terrible.

Thousands of people in this city came from Poland or have relatives there. You should write about events in the world that are important to the people who live in this city.

KRYSTYNA MICHALEK

LOVE PARK—Last week was National Volunteer Week, but there was nothing about it in the newspaper. Many people give their time, energy, money, and love to help other people. They don't ask for recognition, but I think other people should know about them. I think you should write some stories about the interesting volunteers in this city. I sure hope you remember this next year when it's National Volunteer Week again.

JOAN SHIPLEY

Exercise 7: What are the main ideas of the two letters? Write them on the lines and share them with a partner.

1. Krystyna Michalek:  _____

2. Joan Shipley: _____

Exercise 8: With a group talk about letters to editors of newspapers.

Discuss these questions or think of your own questions.
Which letter was most interesting to you? Why?
Do you agree with either or both of the letters? Why or why not?
Why do you think people wrote those letters?
Have you ever written a letter to a newspaper? Why? What happened?

Exercise 9: Write your own letter to a newspaper editor about something that happened recently or something you think newspapers should write about. Share your letter with the class.

WRAP-UP

With a group brainstorm a list of world problems on a sheet of paper. Then choose one problem and think of as many solutions to the problem as you can. Make an idea map. Write your ideas in the circles.

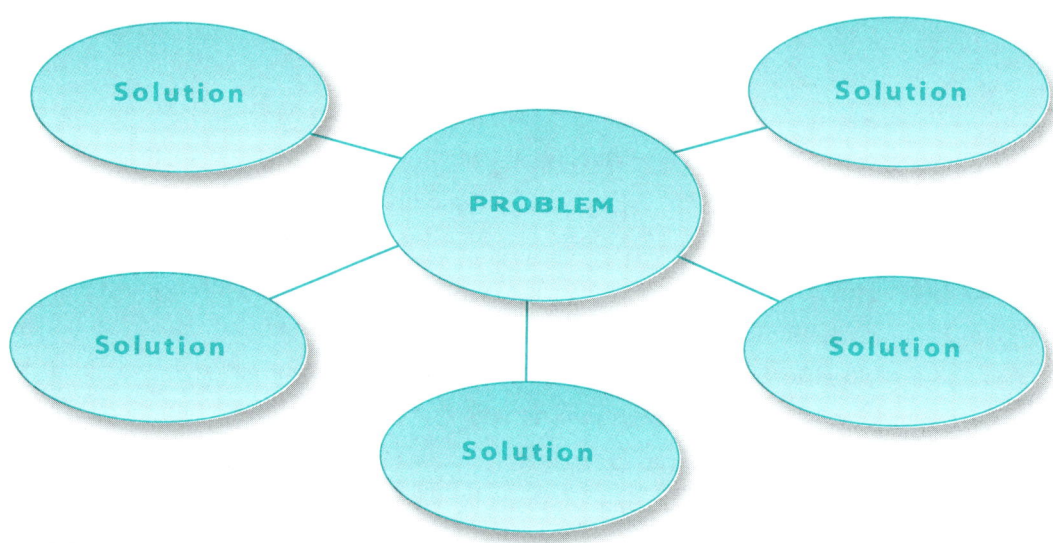

Present your ideas to another group or the class. Use passive-voice verbs, present conditional, and the conditional with *would* in your sentences if you can. Decide if the class should write a letter to the editor of a newspaper in your city.

Think About Learning

In this unit you learned a variety of skills and language structures.
Look at the items below and check how easy or difficult each one was for you.
At the bottom write one other thing you learned.

SKILLS / STRUCTURES	Page	easy ☺	so-so 😐	difficult ☹
Talk about people's problems	25			
Understand recorded conversations	26			
Read a memo and a thank-you note	29			
Talk about how people help others	30			
Read a bar graph and a map	34			
Read and write letters to the editor	35			
Brainstorm ideas about a problem and present your ideas	36			
Use passive verbs	27			
Use present conditionals	32			
Use conditionals with *would*	33			

UNIT 4 ALTERNATIVE MEDICINE AND HEALTHY LIVING

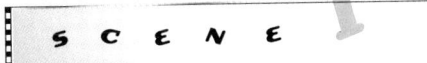

Read the comic strip with a partner. Ask each other the questions below. Then share your answers with another pair or the class.

Jay and Kamal are working in a factory.

FACTS	What's the problem? What are Jay and Kamal talking about? What is alternative medicine?
FEELINGS	How does Kamal feel?
AND YOU?	Have you ever had bad side effects from medicine? Explain what happened.
COMPARISONS	Do you go to the doctor more or less often than you did in your native country? Explain your reasons.
ACTIONS	What should Kamal do? What do you think will happen next?

Now write or tell the story in your own words.

VOCABULARY PROMPTS

Before you listen, talk about the words below in small groups.

acupuncture　　chiropractor　　enroll　　claim

SOUND BITES

Look at the pictures and read about the people's problems.

While You Listen　Listen to the three recordings and write the number each person should press for help. You will hear each recording twice.

1.
Alternative Medicine Group

Problem: You have very bad allergies.

Press: _____

Problem: You have lower-back pain.

Press: _____

2.
Family Doctor Center

Problem: Your daughter is sick. You want to ask the nurse if she needs to see the doctor.

Press: _____

Problem: Your two-year-old just drank from a bottle of floor cleaner.

Press: _____

3.
Atlantic HMO

Problem: You want to join the health plan, but you don't know where to begin.

Press: _____

Problem: You think your medical bill is wrong.

Press: _____

SPOTLIGHT ON GERUNDS

Living with allergies isn't easy.

Taking this medicine makes me sleepy.

A gerund is the *-ing* form of the verb that is used as a noun.
You can use gerunds as the subject of a sentence.

You keep **getting** sick, don't you?
Have you thought of **trying** acupuncture?

Gerunds can also come after certain verbs or prepositions.

Exercise 1: In pairs read the Nutrition Quiz below. Are the statements true or false? Circle T or F. Compare your answers with the class.

How Much Do You Know About Nutrition?

1.	Eating fruits and vegetables every day can keep you from getting cancer.	T F
2.	Nutritionists suggest using dark greens in salads because they have more vitamins than light greens.	T F
3.	Canning fruits and vegetables makes them lose most of their nutritional value.	T F
4.	Frying foods always makes them higher in fat.	T F
5.	Cooking with margarine is no better for you than cooking with butter.	T F
6.	Reading food labels is important because the ingredients are listed in alphabetical order.	T F
7.	Being overweight makes you more at risk for cancer.	T F

Your Turn

In small groups make a list of ways to stay healthy. Use gerunds wherever possible. Do different cultures have different ideas about nutrition? Discuss this question with the class.

Person to Person

Listen to these conversations. With a partner finish the last conversation.
Then practice the conversations with your partner.

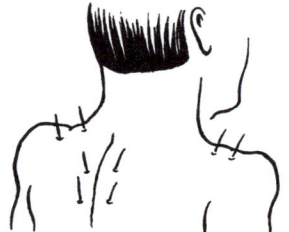

KAMAL: What is acupuncture?

DOCTOR: Putting needles in parts of your body to help with conditions like asthma.

KAMAL: Does it hurt when you put the needle in?

DOCTOR: No. It feels like a mosquito bite.

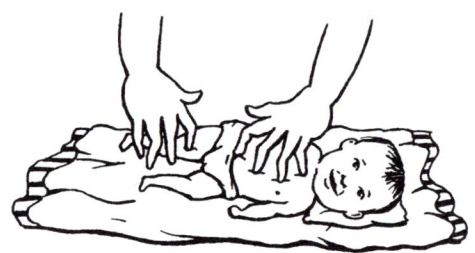

SUE: What are you doing?

EVA: My baby was born one month early. Our doctor told us to try massaging him every day.

SUE: What does that do?

EVA: It helps him to eat and to gain weight.

SUE: And he seems to like it too!

JAN: You look great!

PETE: I've just come back from the chiropractor. My back feels 100 percent better.

JAN: I have back problems too. Should I think about seeing a chiropractor?

PETE: Yes. It feels great to move around without any back pain!

KATE: Weren't you sick the other day?

MIKE: Yes, but not now.

KATE: What did you do?

MIKE: I took some natural medicine.

_____

Your Turn

With a partner write a conversation about a health problem. You can use
ideas from the lists you made on page 39. Use gerunds wherever possible.
Share your conversation with the class.

In small groups talk about the words below.

provider   (in)eligible   covered   HMO   PCP

READING FOR REAL

Kamal received a statement from his health plan. Read the statement.

HEALTHSOURCE HMO P.O. BOX 209
1400 CENTER ST.
CEDARVILLE, WI 54702

DATE: 2/7/99
PATIENT NO.: 306-48-2107-3C
PATIENT: KAMAL PATEL

DATE OF BENEFIT SERVICE	TYPE OF SERVICE	PROVIDER	CHARGED AMOUNT	INELIGIBLE AMOUNT	COVERED AMOUNT	ELIGIBLE AMOUNT
12/6/98	PCP VISIT	FAMILY DOCTOR HMO	85.00	00.00	85.00	85.00
12/8/98	PRESCR. MED.	WALNUT DRUGS	17.00	3.00	14.00	14.00
1/15/99	ACU-PUNCT.	ALTERN. MED. GR.	175.00	175.00	00.00	00.00
		COLUMN TOTALS	277.00	178.00	99.00	99.00

TOTAL CHARGED AMOUNT   277.00
TOTAL COVERED   99.00
PAID BY OTHER PLAN   00.00
TO BE PAID BY YOU   178.00

THIS IS AN EXPLANATION OF COVERAGE

Exercise 2: In groups of two or three, write answers to the questions below.

1. What is the name of Kamal's health plan? _____

2. When did Kamal see his PCP (primary care physician)? _____

3. How much did the health plan pay for Kamal's prescription? _____

4. How much did the health plan pay for the acupuncture? _____

5. Can Kamal do anything about the bill? _____

In Your Experience

Have you ever had problems with a medical bill? What did you do?
Discuss the problem in small groups and share it with the class.
Talk about common problems with medical bills and ways to solve them.

CULTURE CORNER

Read the article about alternative medicine below.

Alternative Medicine: Is It Effective?

What Some Western Doctors Say

Alternative medicine is becoming more popular in the United States. Some insurance companies have agreed to pay for alternative treatments. This is what some Western doctors think about four types of alternative medicine.

1. **Acupuncture** This is the ancient practice of putting needles in certain parts of the body to help with all kinds of problems. Some doctors even use acupuncture so that people can stay awake during major operations. There is not much scientific proof about acupuncture, but it can be good for stopping pain and treating chronic (long-term) conditions such as back pain or asthma.

2. **Aromatherapy** Smells affect how we feel. Some people use oils from flowers, roots, bark, and leaves to stay healthy. They spray, breathe, and bathe in the scents. Aromatherapy probably won't help with serious illnesses, but it can help to relax you and to treat skin conditions.

3. **Ayurveda** This system of healing comes from India. It means "knowledge of life." Ayurveda combines nutrition and meditation to keep people "in balance" with their environment. There is no evidence that Ayurveda will stop disease, but it can help you to lead a healthier life.

4. **Chiropractics** Chiropractors believe that they can stop disease and pain by putting people's backbones in the correct position. Going to a chiropractor may not be better than going to a regular doctor, but many people are happy with their chiropractic treatment. Make sure your chiropractor has a license.

Your Turn

In small groups talk about the four different kinds of alternative medicine. Describe how they work. According to Western doctors, how effective is each kind of treatment?

Think about Kamal's medical bill on page 41. Why do you think the health plan refused to pay for the acupuncture?

In Your Experience

Have you tried (or would you try) alternative medicine? If so, what kind? In small groups discuss your experiences and opinions. Do a class survey to find out how many students are in favor of which treatment.

SCENE 2

Read the comic strip with a partner. Ask each other the questions below.
Then share your answers with another pair or the class.

Kamal has received a big bill for his acupuncture visit.

FACTS	What's the problem? Who is Kamal talking to? What does he want?
FEELINGS	How does Kamal feel?
AND YOU?	Have you ever felt frustrated about health problems?
COMPARISONS	Do many people belong to health plans in your native country? Can most people get the health care they need?
ACTIONS	What do you think Kamal should do? What will happen next?

VOCABULARY PROMPTS

Before you listen, talk about the words below in small groups.

reimbursement form   specialist   referral   network

SOUND BITES

While You Listen Listen for the answers to the questions and take notes.
How does Kamal feel? Why? What does he want?
What is the customer service person telling him?

SPOTLIGHT ON INFINITIVES

You need **to see** your primary doctor.
I decided **to talk** to my doctor about my medication.
I refused **to take** the medicine.
My doctor agreed **to change** the dosage.

Infinitives come after certain verbs.

I reminded <u>my doctor</u> **to write** a referral
The nurse told <u>me</u> **to make** an appointment.
She encouraged <u>me</u> **to ask** about alternative treatments.

When the verb involves another person, the noun or pronoun comes
between the verb and the infinitive.

Exercise 3: Look at the list of infinitives and read the passage below.
Then write the correct infinitive in each sentence. There may be more
than one correct answer.

to get   to make   to do   to have   to see   to go

Sometimes parents are very stubborn. My father needed (1) __to get/to have__

a knee operation. I encouraged him (2) _____ a doctor.

He refused (3) _____ help. He didn't want

(4) _____ an operation. I finally convinced him

(5) _____ an appointment. The doctor told him

(6) _____ to the hospital right away. He finally agreed

(7) _____ the operation. After the operation the nurse

reminded my father (8) _____ his knee exercises every day.

Now my father walks better than ever!

In Your Experience

Do you know someone who doesn't like doctors? With a partner talk about this
person. Use verbs such as *need to, want to, refuse to, encourage (someone) to,*
and *convince (someone) to.* Write a short paragraph about the person and share
it with a group or the class.

SPOTLIGHT ON GERUNDS AND INFINITIVES

Don't delay **getting** your flu shot!
I appreciate **having** insurance.
I want to talk to a doctor instead of **listening** to a recording.

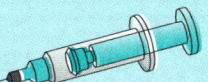

Some verbs (or prepositions) are followed by gerunds.

If you need **to order** a schedule of classes, press 3.
I want **to see** the nurse.
You are required **to show** some ID.

Other verbs are followed by infinitives.

Please continue **holding**.
Please continue **to hold**.
I started **feeling** dizzy.
I started **to feel** dizzy.

Certain verbs can be followed by either a gerund or an infinitive.

Exercise 4: First read the passage below. Then complete each sentence with a gerund or infinitive. With a partner compare your answers.

Seeing a doctor in the United States is very different from (1) *see* _____ one in my native country. In my native country, we pay a doctor when we're sick instead of (2) *join* _____ health plans and (3) *have* _____ insurance. When I started (4) *work* _____ in the United States, my company told me (5) *choose* _____ between two different health plans.

I joined an HMO, and I appreciate (6) *have* _____ so many services in one place. If I want (7) *make* _____ an appointment for myself and my son, I can have both in the same hour. There are some disadvantages, however.

If I need (8) *speak* _____ to a nurse, sometimes I have to wait a long time.

We are also required (9) *get* _____ a referral to see any specialists.

GET GRAPHIC

Study the chart below.

U.S. GENDER STATISTICS IN THE LATE 1990s

Leading Causes of Death in the United States		Leading Causes of Death by Race and Gender (45 to 64 yrs.)	
CAUSE	**DEATHS**	**WHITE FEMALE**	**BLACK FEMALE**
1. Heart disease	739,000	1. Cancer	1. Cancer
2. Cancer	538,000	2. Heart disease	2. Heart disease
3. Stroke	158,000	3. Lung disorders	3. Stroke
4. Lung disorders	105,000	**WHITE MALE**	**BLACK MALE**
5. Accidents	90,000	1. Heart disease	1. Heart disease
6. Pneumonia and flu	84,000	2. Cancer	2. Cancer
7. Diabetes	59,000	3. Accidents	3. AIDS

Exercise 5: Work in small groups. Match the letters with the numbers.

1. gender _____   a. blood blocked in the brain

2. leading cause _____   b. illness in which the body's sugar is not balanced

3. stroke _____   c. male or female

4. pneumonia _____   d. illness in which the lungs are infected

5. diabetes _____   e. the most common reason

Exercise 6: In groups of two or three, decide if each statement below is *true* or *false*.

1. More Americans died from heart disease than from any other cause. _____true_____

2. Fewer people died from cancer than from stroke. _____

3. In general, more women die of cancer than of heart disease. _____

4. Heart disease is the leading cause of death for men. _____

5. Drunk driving is the number one killer in the United States. _____

In Your Experience

What illnesses and diseases do you worry about? In the same groups of two or three, talk about your concerns. Make a list, discuss reasons, and share your ideas with the class. With the class make a graph to show which illnesses worry everyone the most.

ISSUES AND ANSWERS

Many U.S. companies have a "suggestion box" for employees to write about ideas or problems at work. Read the suggestions and answer below. Write an answer to Sandra's and Jorge's suggestions.

SUGGESTION

I don't understand the changes on my paycheck. Why does the employee contribution keep going up? I would like someone to explain that to me.

JOE,
SHIPPING AND RECEIVING

ANSWER

There are changes mainly because of the rising cost of health care. Everything gets more expensive each year. We're having a meeting about benefits on December 1. Try to attend, or stop by my office with specific questions.

EVELYN,
PERSONNEL

SUGGESTION

Can we have some healthier food in the cafeteria? My doctor told me to eat less fat, salt, and cholesterol, but there aren't many good choices on the menu. It would also be nice to have a way to exercise during breaks at work.

SANDRA,
ACCOUNTING

ANSWER

_____

_____

_____

_____

_____

SUGGESTION

I'm very concerned about the air in the factory. It's very hot, and the smell of the plastic gives me headaches. There are fans, but they don't help much. I suggest getting a better air system as soon as possible.

JORGE,
VINYL DEPT.

ANSWER

_____

_____

_____

_____

_____

Then write your own suggestion or problem on an index card. Use gerunds and infinitives wherever you can. Put the suggestions in a box and have students pick a card and write a response. Share with the class.

WRAP-UP

With the class or in small groups, use a Venn diagram like the one below to think about medicine or nutrition in your native country and the United States. For example, how are hospitals, doctors, or treatments different from those in the United States? How are they the same?

MEDICINE AND NUTRITION

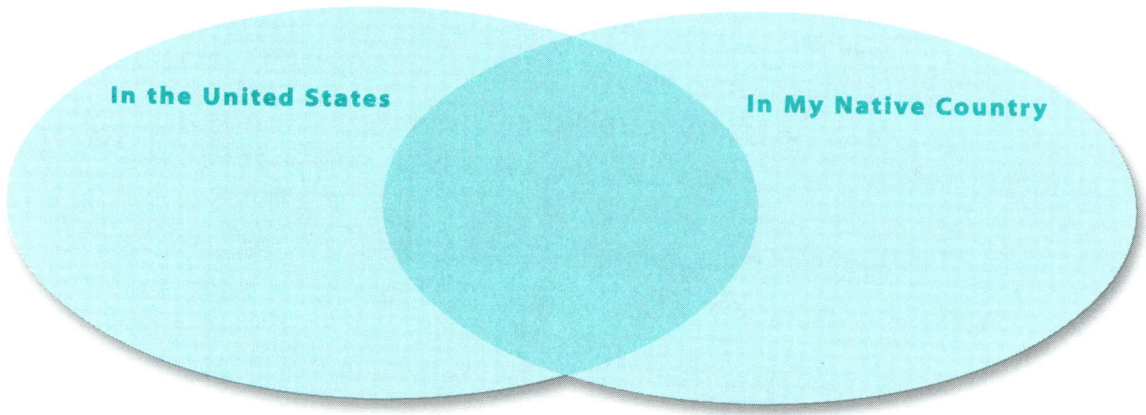

In the United States

In My Native Country

Share your diagram with the class. Then, in your groups, write a short paragraph about how medicine is the same or different in your cultures. Use gerunds and infinitives. Work with the class to make a health newsletter. Include some healthy recipes if you can!

Think About Learning
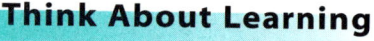

In this unit you learned a variety of skills and language structures. Look at the items below and check how easy or difficult each one was for you. At the bottom write one other thing you learned.

SKILLS / STRUCTURES	Page	easy ☺	so-so ☺	difficult ☹
Talk about health problems	37			
Understand medical recordings	38			
Understand alternative medicine and health insurance	42			
Read a medical statement	41			
Interpret a chart with health statistics	46			
Read and write suggestions	47			
Use an idea map about health in different cultures	48			
Use gerunds and infinitives	39, 44, 45			

CITIZENSHIP AND DOCUMENTATION FOR WORK

Read the comic strip with a partner. Ask each other the questions below. Then share your answers with another pair or the class.

Monique is going to take her citizenship test.

FACTS	What's the problem? What is Monique doing?
FEELINGS	How does she feel?
AND YOU?	Have you ever felt scared or nervous before a test? Explain.
COMPARISONS	What does a person have to do to become a citizen of your native country?
ACTIONS	What should Monique do? What do you think will happen next?

Now write or tell the story in your own words.

VOCABULARY PROMPTS

Before you listen, talk about the words below in small groups.

permanent resident   retire   approve   dual citizenship

SOUND BITES

Some of Monique's co-workers are asking friends for advice about citizenship.

While You Listen In your notebook take notes on the conversations.

1. Stana wants to apply for citizenship.

   She should ___wait two years___.

3. Crispin is afraid to take the citizenship

   test. He ought to _____.

5. Jaime has a problem with his fingerprints.

   He has to _____.

2. Han doesn't know the advantages of being a

   citizen. He should _____.

4. Canan needs help with her forms.

   She had better _____.

6. Beatriz isn't sure she wants to become a U.S.

   citizen. She should _____.

After You Listen In groups of three, compare your notes and help write
the advice for each situation. Share your advice with another group.

Your Turn

In your notebook write a sentence about another problem or question
about citizenship. Read it to your group and get advice.

SPOTLIGHT ON MODALS OF ADVICE AND NECESSITY

Advice

Here's a good idea...

You **should** wait another two years before applying for citizenship.

You **ought to** take a citizenship class.

You**'d better** get some help.

Necessity

Do this!

You **have to** be a permanent resident for five years.

You **must** be able to read, speak, and write English to pass the test.

You**'ve got to** find out where to take the exam.

Exercise 1: With a partner, match Column A with Column B. Write the correct letter on the line.

COLUMN A

1. I want to apply for citizenship. _____

2. I want to learn to speak English better. _____

3. There's a strange noise when I start my car. _____

4. I want to take a math class. _____

5. I haven't spoken to my family in six years. _____

6. I'm taking prescription medicine. _____

COLUMN B

a. You'd better take it to a mechanic.

b. You've got to sign up for a placement test first.

c. You shouldn't drink alcohol.

d. You ought to call them.

e. You have to be a permanent resident for five years.

f. You should practice outside class as much as possible.

In Your Experience

Look at Exercise 1 and circle situations you have been in from Column A. Then compare your circles with those of your partner and ask for advice about those situations.

Person to Person

Listen to these conversations. With a partner finish the last conversation.
Use modals of advice and necessity wherever possible. Then practice
the conversations with your partner.

CHOEN: Can anyone become President of the
         United States?

LISA: No, you must be at least 35 years old.

CHOEN: I'm 35!

LISA: And you must be a native-born citizen.

CHOEN: Oh well.

CUSTOMER: Hey! I was next!

EMPLOYEE: Are you number 62?

CUSTOMER: I didn't know I needed a number.

EMPLOYEE: Sorry, you'll have to take a number
            and wait your turn.

CUSTOMER: I can't believe this!

ANNA: Shouldn't your daughter be in her car seat?

JENNY: We aren't going very far.

ANNA: What if we get into an accident?

JENNY: You're right. I guess I'd better pull over
         and put her in the car seat.

AHMED: I won't be able to go out this weekend.

MIKE: Why?

AHMED: I've got to work overtime on Saturday
         and Sunday.

MIKE: _____

Your Turn

With a partner write a conversation about a problem situation.
Try to use modals of advice and necessity. Share your conversation
with a group or the class.

VOCABULARY PROMPTS

In small groups talk about the words below.

naturalization   petition   barred   oath

READING FOR REAL

Before Monique applied for citizenship, she read these requirements.
Read them carefully. Then, with the class discuss the meaning of each requirement.

REQUIREMENTS FOR NATURALIZATION

1. You must be at least 18 years old.

2. You must be a lawful permanent resident of the United States.

3. You must reside in the United States continuously as a lawful permanent resident for five years before filing a naturalization petition.

4. You must demonstrate that you are of good moral character during the required residence period.

5. You cannot have been a member of the Communist Party for a 10-year period before petitioning for naturalization.

6. If you are a deserter from the U. S. armed forces or were discharged from the U.S. armed forces for this reason, you are permanently barred from naturalization.

7. You must be able to speak, read, write, and understand simple English and pass a test on U.S. history and government. Persons over 50 who have been legal permanent residents for 20 years do not need to take the literacy test.

8. You must take an oath of allegiance to the United States.

Exercise 2: In groups of two or three, write *true* or *false* next to each statement below. Explain why each answer is correct.

1. Anyone can apply for citizenship. _____

2. A small child cannot apply for citizenship. _____

3. Someone who was a Communist 20 years ago can still become a citizen. _____

4. If you run away from the U.S. Army, you can never become a citizen. _____

5. If your English is very good, you do not need to study U.S. history and

   government for the test. _____

In Your Experience

Can *you* apply for citizenship? Discuss this question with a group.

VOCABULARY PROMPTS

In small groups talk about the words below.

INS   courting   sponsor   public charge   reunited

CULTURE CORNER

The story in this article is true. Read the article.

MARRIED COUPLE SEPARATED BECAUSE OF INS RULES

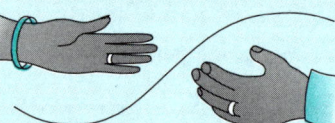

Evelyn Ellis and Jonathan McLeary met 50 years ago in Jamaica. She was only 16 and said no to his wedding proposal. Then, just a few years ago, they met in Canada while Evelyn was visiting family. Jonathan started courting Evelyn. After she returned to her home in the United States, he sent her romantic cassette tapes and letters. Finally, at ages 67 and 73, Evelyn and Jonathan were married. According to friends, Evelyn's life changed, and she seemed much happier and years younger.

Then the bad news came. Evelyn lives on SSI (Social Security Income). The INS told her she was too poor to sponsor Jonathan for permanent residency in the United States. Also, Jonathan went to the hospital for a blood clot and couldn't pay the $7,000 bill. INS procedures do not allow people who can't pay their bills to become permanent residents.

So Jonathan had to return to Canada, where he receives financial assistance from the government. On Valentine's Day he sent Evelyn a card. A phone call was too expensive. Jonathan says it's very hard to be so far away from his wife. But Evelyn says she knows now what love is, and her religion keeps her strong. They are still hoping that their case will be reviewed again by the INS. They hope to be reunited again.

Exercise 3: Discuss the questions below in small groups.

Why did Evelyn and Jonathan have problems with INS?

Do you think Jonathan should be allowed to become a permanent resident?

Do a class survey. How many people say yes, and how many say no?

In Your Experience

Think about a situation in your personal life that was affected by rules and regulations. Talk with a partner or write a short paragraph about the situation.

Read the comic strip with a partner. Ask each other the questions below.
Then share your answers with another pair or the class.

Monique is starting her oral interview.

FACTS	What happened in the interview? Has Monique been outside of the United States since she arrived in the country?
FEELINGS	How does Monique feel? Who is she thinking about?
AND YOU?	Have you ever felt the way Monique does?
COMPARISONS	In your native country can immigrants become citizens?
ACTIONS	What advice do you have for Monique?

VOCABULARY PROMPTS

Before you listen, talk about the words below in small groups.

raid   arrested   deported   pay a fine

SOUND BITES

While You Listen Take notes and listen for the answers to the questions.
What happened at the plant? What might happen to Philippe and the
other workers? What will happen to the company?

SPOTLIGHT ON SHORT ANSWERS

Did you pass your citizenship test?   Yes, I **did.**

Are you working full-time?   Yes, I **am.**

Do you get benefits?   No, I **don't.**

Is that a problem for you?   Yes, it **is.**

Have you talked to your boss about it?   No, I **haven't.**

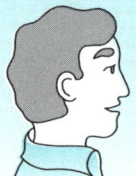 

Exercise 4:   Look at Monique's application for citizenship. Give short answers to the examiner's questions below. Then practice your questions and answers with a partner.

U.S. DEPARTMENT OF JUSTICE		APPLICATION FOR NATURALIZATION
IMMIGRATION AND NATURALIZATION SERVICE		

START HERE - Please Type or Print

Part 1. Information about you.

Family Name DuValle	Given Name Monique	Middle Initial J

U.S. Mailing Address— Care of Maria DuValle

Street Number and Name   216 W. Clark St.   Apt. #   3

City Chicago   County Cook   State Illinois   Zip Code 60652

Date of Birth (Month/day/year) 9/26/77   Country of Birth   Haiti

Social Security #   444-36-1381

Date you became a permanent resident (month/day/year) 2/21/90

Sex: ___Male X Female	Height:	Marital Status: X Single ___ Married	___ Divorced ___ Widowed

Can you speak, read, and write English?   ___ No   X Yes

EXAMINER: Is your family name DuValle?

MONIQUE: _Yes it is._____

EXAMINER: Were you born in 1977?

MONIQUE: _____

EXAMINER: Is Haiti your native country?

MONIQUE: _____

EXAMINER: Are you a permanent resident?

MONIQUE: _____

EXAMINER: Can you speak, read, and write English?

MONIQUE: _____

EXAMINER: Are you married?

MONIQUE: _____

Your Turn

With a partner ask and answer questions like the ones above.
Give your own information.

SPOTLIGHT ON TAG ENDINGS

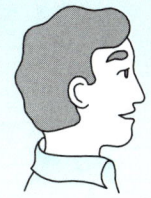

You **passed** your citizenship test,	**didn't** you?
You**'re** working full-time,	**aren't** you?
You **don't** get benefits,	**do** you?
That**'s** a problem for you,	**isn't** it?
You **haven't** talked to your boss about it,	**have** you?

You can use *tag endings* when you think you know the answer, but you want to be sure.
If the verb is positive, the tag is negative. If the verb is negative, the tag is positive.

Exercise 5: Use *tag endings* to check your understanding
of these work situations.

1. We're supposed to hand in these forms, ___*aren't we*___ ?

2. This is the reset button, _____?

3. We can't smoke in here, _____?

4. There's a law against forced overtime, _____?

5. It isn't time for break yet, _____?

6. We don't have to work on Labor Day, _____?

Exercise 6: With a partner fill in
the blanks with appropriate tag
endings or questions. Then practice
the conversations by moving around
the classroom and making small talk.

Small talk is conversation about the weather and unimportant things. Americans use small talk to be polite and find something to say.

1. You were out sick, ___*weren't you*___ ?

   Yes, I ___*was*___.

2. You're from Guatemala, _____?

   _____

3. It's (hot/cold/stuffy) in here, _____?

   _____

4. You got a haircut, _____?

   _____

GET GRAPHIC

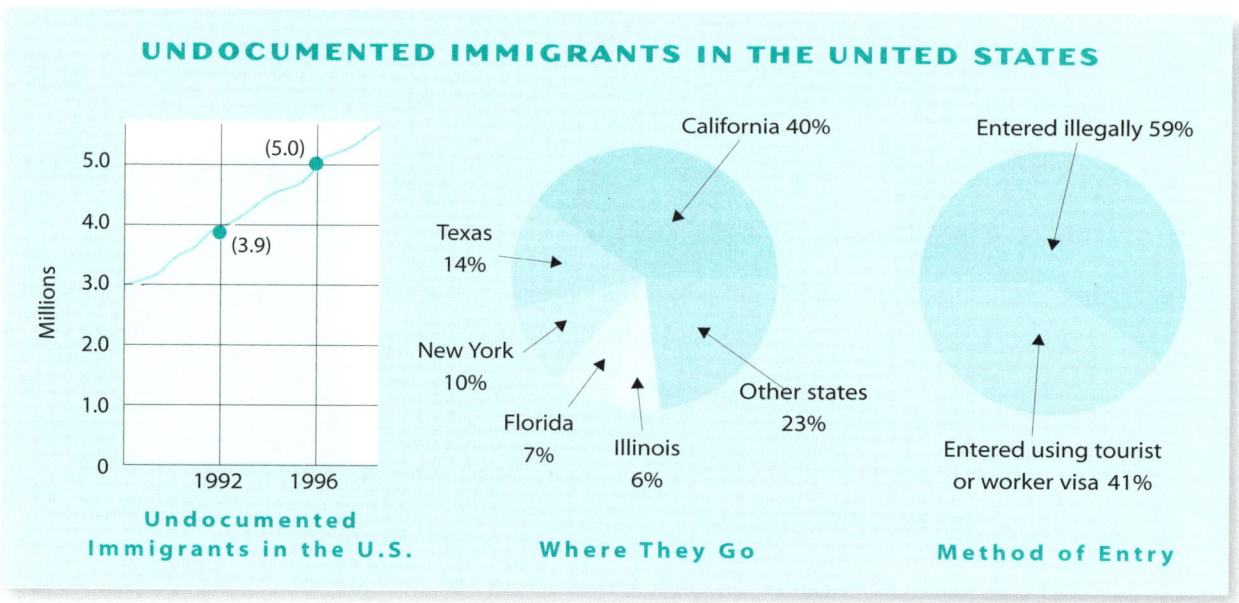

UNDOCUMENTED IMMIGRANTS IN THE UNITED STATES

Millions — (5.0), (3.9) — 1992, 1996

Undocumented Immigrants in the U.S.

California 40%
Texas 14%
New York 10%
Florida 7%
Illinois 6%
Other states 23%

Where They Go

Entered illegally 59%
Entered using tourist or worker visa 41%

Method of Entry

 Exercise 7: In pairs match the words in Column A with the meanings in Column B.

COLUMN A

1. increase   _____
2. fair   _____
3. undocumented   _____
4. percent   _____
5. visa   _____

COLUMN B

a. without papers, illegal
b. temporary traveling permit
c. just, equal
d. part of 100
e. go up

  Exercise 8: Look at the graph and pie charts. Write *true* or *false* for each statement below.

1. Between 1992 and 1996 the number of undocumented immigrants increased. ___*true*___

2. California is the state with the largest percentage of undocumented immigrants. _____

3. California has more undocumented immigrants than all of the other states combined. _____

4. Most undocumented immigrants entered the country with a tourist or worker visa. _____

  Talk About It

In groups talk about the following questions. If others disagree with your ideas, try to defend your point of view.

Why do you think people come to or stay in the United States illegally?

What risks do they take? Are the benefits worth the risk?

What is a fair government policy for undocumented immigrants?

ISSUES AND ANSWERS

Read the e-mail message below.

E-Mail Message — ☐ ✕

From: isleb@genco.inc **Date: Thurs, 14 Aug 8:42:10**
To: lkent@hillcoll.edu **Subject: Need help**

Lisa: Thanks for your last e-mail. Sorry I haven't written in so long. I miss being in your English class since I moved. I like my new town. I'm working in a factory called Genco. Things are fine here, but I need to make some decisions. I've lived in this country for so long, but I've never voted. I know the United States is my home, but somehow I've never really felt like an American. Do you think I should become a citizen? I'm not sure what I have to do to apply. What do you think I should do? Write back soon.

Fondly, Inga

From: lkent@hillcoll.edu **Date: Fri, 15 Aug 15:32:02**
To: isleb@genco.inc **Subject: Some advice**

_____

_____

_____

_____

Take care, Lisa

Exercise 9: Answer the questions below with a partner.

Is there a way to find out Inga's and Lisa's last names?
Who is e-mailing from a company? Who is e-mailing from a school?
How do Inga and Lisa know each other? What is Inga trying to decide?
How does she feel?

Your Turn

Write Lisa's response to Inga. Then, in your notebook write an e-mail message to a friend and have a partner respond. Use modals of advice and necessity, short answers, and tag endings wherever possible.

WRAP-UP

With the class or in small groups, use this T-chart to list some problems that undocumented people face. Then brainstorm solutions to those problems. You do not need to write complete sentences.

PROBLEMS FOR UNDOCUMENTED PEOPLE	SOLUTIONS TO THE PROBLEMS

Now, in pairs or small groups write a short article about the problems of undocumented people to go into a student newspaper. First describe the problems. Then suggest some solutions.

Think About Learning

In this unit you learned a variety of skills and language structures. Look at the items below and check how easy or difficult each one was for you. At the bottom write one other thing you learned.

SKILLS / STRUCTURES	Page	easy ☺	so-so 😐	difficult ☹
Talk about people's problems	49			
Understand conversations	52			
Understand citizenship requirements	53			
Read an article	54			
Understand line graphs, pie charts	58			
Solve problems through writing	59			
Brainstorm and write an article	60			
Use modals of advice and necessity	51			
Use short answers	56			
Use tag endings	57			

ENTERTAINMENT AND THE ARTS

SCENE 1

Read the comic strip with a partner. Ask each other the questions below. Then share your answers with another pair or the class.

Victoria has wanted to be a dancer since she was a little girl.

FACTS	What's the problem? When did Victoria decide to be a dancer?
FEELINGS	How does Victoria feel about dancing? How does she feel about her injury?
AND YOU?	Were you ever stopped from accomplishing your goals or dreams? What happened?
COMPARISONS	Do you know any people who are dancers? What kind of dancing is popular in your country?
ACTIONS	What do you think will happen to Victoria?

Now write or tell the story in your own words.

Before you listen, talk about these words in a group.

fascinating   boring   mystery   thrilling   event

SOUND BITES

Listen to the conversations between co-workers about entertainment.

While You Listen   Listen to the conversations and fill in the chart below.

CONVERSATION	WHAT IS/WAS THE EVENT?	WHEN IS/WAS IT?	WHAT WORD DESCRIBES IT?
1. Lydia and Kathryn are talking at lunch about their weekend.			
2. Jan and Mark are talking about their weekend during break.			
3. Barb and Julie are walking on their lunch hour.			
4. Tom and Anthony are waiting for the bus after work.			

After You Listen   Talk to a partner about the events in the chart. Decide which one is the most interesting to you. Give reasons. Share your answers with the class.

Your Turn

Think about who you talk to at work or at school. Make a list of the people you talk to and the things you talk about on break or while eating lunch or dinner. Share your list with a partner.

SPOTLIGHT ON PRESENT PARTICIPLES AS ADJECTIVES

Flamenco is a **fascinating** dance. = Flamenco fascinates (someone).

The soccer game was **boring**. = The soccer game bored (someone).

This is an **interesting** game. = This game interests (someone).

Present participles used as adjectives describe nouns or pronouns.
The present participle describes the cause of the feeling.

Exercise 1: Use the present participles as adjectives below
to complete the sentences about entertainment.

amazing	confusing	entertaining	surprising
annoying	disappointing	exhausting	thrilling
boring	embarrassing	frustrating	tiring

JOHN: I saw an (1) _____ performance by the *Ballet Folklórico
de Mexico* on Sunday. The dancers were terrific, and the costumes were
(2) _____.

ANNA: That was a (3) _____ TV show.
The story didn't make sense, and it was (4) _____.

KEESHA: I went to a (5) _____ basketball game last night.
The first three quarters were (6) _____ because the
players made a lot of mistakes. The fans booed at the teams'
(7) _____ performance.

DAN: I used to think country-western music was (8) _____.
But a month ago I went to a country-western dance club. I danced
and sang and laughed all night. It was (9) _____,
but what an (10) _____ night.

Your Turn

Think about shows and events you have seen recently and your opinions
of them. Write three to five sentences using present participles as adjectives
from the list above. Share your sentences with a partner. For example,
write, "I saw an exciting soccer game last night."

Person to Person

One good topic of small talk at work is entertainment. Listen to these co-workers' conversations. With a partner, finish the last conversation. Use present participles as adjectives if you can. Then practice the conversations with your partner.

SUE: Did you watch TV last night?

JANE: No. I couldn't find any interesting programs to watch. How about you?

SUE: I watched an amazing show about tigers on the Discovery Channel.

JANE: I wish I had cable TV.

LAURA: Would you like to go to a movie after work on Thursday?

ROSE: I'd love to, but I can't. My dance class is on Thursday.

LAURA: I didn't know you took a dance class.

ROSE: Yeah. I love to dance. It's good exercise, and it's very relaxing.

HECTOR: What did you think of the movie?

TOMAS: The acting was disappointing.

HECTOR: I thought the story was confusing too.

TOMAS: I agree. I didn't like the movie at all.

HECTOR: Next time we should read a review first.

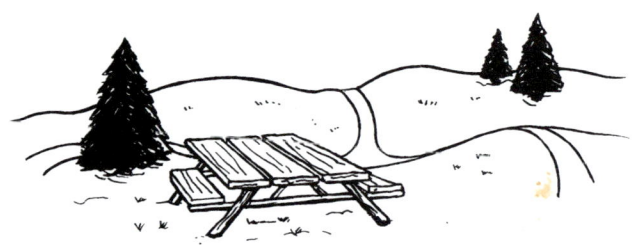

SAM: Are you going to the company picnic?

ED: I don't think so. Last year it was so boring. There wasn't a lot to do.

SAM: _____

ED: _____

Your Turn

With a partner write a conversation about something you talked about with a classmate or a co-worker recently. Include opinions using present participles as adjectives. Share your conversation with a group or the class.

Before you read the brochure below, talk about these words in a group.

postmodern   ethnic   rhythmic   subscribe

READING FOR REAL

Victoria and her friends want to go to a dance performance.
Read the dance performance brochure below.

PROGRAM 1

MODERN DANCE FESTIVAL

This show includes thrilling new moves and bold new ideas.

FRIDAY, OCTOBER 24, and
WEDNESDAY, NOVEMBER 19,
at 8:00 P.M. **$15**

PROGRAM 2

INTERNATIONAL DANCE FESTIVAL

Scottish, Egyptian, Polish, and Russian dancers are featured in this fascinating evening of dance.

SUNDAY, OCTOBER 26,
SUNDAY, NOVEMBER 2, and
SUNDAY, NOVEMBER, 23
at 3:00 P.M.

$15

PROGRAM 3

FEEL THE BEAT!

The dances include tap, flamenco, drum storytelling, and Irish step dance.

SATURDAY, NOVEMBER 1,
WEDNESDAY, NOVEMBER 12,
and FRIDAY, NOVEMBER 21,
at 8:00 P.M. **$15**

TICKET ORDER FORM

PROGRAM NUMBER _____

QUANTITY _____

PRICE _____

TOTAL _____

Order tickets to different programs and get a discount.

2 DIFFERENT PROGRAMS—
$12.00 each

3 DIFFERENT PROGRAMS—
$10.00 each

SUBSCRIBE BY FAX (925-555-6879)
or BY PHONE (925-555-6880)

Exercise 2: Answer *true* or *false*.

1. The ticket prices for the Sunday dances are more expensive than tickets for other days. _____

2. All the performances are on the weekend. _____

3. Sunday performances are at 3:00 P.M. _____

4. You can see flamenco dancers in Feel the Beat. _____

5. If Victoria and three friends see only one program, the total cost of their tickets will be $15.00. _____

Talk About It

Which performance would you like to see? When would you go?
Who would go with you? Fill out the order form above and
talk about it with a partner.

CULTURE CORNER

With the class discuss these questions: What is dancing? Why do people dance? Why are there so many different kinds of dances?

Exercise 3: Complete the chart below. Then share your answers with a group or the class. Talk about the dances in the chart. Ask questions such as these: What kind of dancing is ballet? Who has seen a ballet? Who knows how to do ballet?

NAME OF DANCE	I'VE SEEN IT.	I'VE DONE IT.	I WANT TO LEARN IT.
Ballet			
Belly dancing			
Bharata natya (Hindu temple dancing)			
Country-Western line dancing			
Flamenco			
Kabuki			
Mambo			
Mazurka			
Polka			
Salsa			
Square dancing			
Tango			
Tap dancing			

Your Turn

In a group make a list of dances that aren't listed in the chart above. Put a check next to the dances you know how to do. Show your list to another group. Circle the dances on your list that other people mentioned. Add new dances to your list. Share the list with the class.

In Your Experience

Show or teach the class a dance you know.

SCENE 2

Read the comic strip with a partner. Ask each other the questions below.
Then share your answers with another pair or the class.

Victoria is not a professional dancer anymore.

I'm not injured permanently, Dad!

Yes, but what if this happens again? You'll be an uneducated ex-dancer. Go to college.

I'm fascinated by this class. I'm glad I listened to my father.

If I have to stop dancing someday, I'll have the education to do something else.

FACTS   What's the problem? What does Victoria's father want her to do?

FEELINGS   How does she feel?

AND YOU?   Have you ever had to change your plans? What happened?

COMPARISONS   How is your life different from what you planned?

ACTIONS   What will Victoria be doing ten years from now?

VOCABULARY PROMPTS

Before you listen, talk about the words below.

worried   broken   exhausted   irritated   scream

SOUND BITES

While You Listen Find the answers to these questions. Take notes.
What doesn't Victoria want to do? Why is her father worried?
What can Victoria do if she continues her education?
After You Listen Discuss the answers with a group. With a partner use
the answers to write a conversation. Share it with the class.

SPOTLIGHT ON PAST PARTICIPLES AS ADJECTIVES

Victoria gave her father an **irritated** look.

Pablo was **worried** about his daughter's future.

Victoria needed a **written** prescription from her doctor.

Past participles used as adjectives describe nouns or pronouns. The past participle describes how a person feels, or the condition of something.

For more on these forms, see the Appendix.

Exercise 4: Read Victoria's conversation with her father. Underline the adjectives. Draw an arrow to the nouns or pronouns they describe.

VICTORIA: No, Dad. I don't want to quit dancing. My leg will heal, and I can go back to work.

PABLO: That's not the point. I'm <u>worried</u> about you. Your leg is broken now, but what will happen next?

VICTORIA: Nothing. I was tired, and I fell. It was just a stupid accident.

PABLO: No, it wasn't. You were dancing eight hours a day, and you were exhausted. That will happen again and again.

VICTORIA: You can't see into the future!

PABLO: Yes, I can. I see an uneducated dancer with no future. You must go to college. Then if you can't dance, you can do something else.

VICTORIA: I want to dance. I don't want to do anything else.

PABLO: I understand that. But you need more. Learn how to teach others to dance. Learn how to run a business. Maybe you can open your own dance school some day.

VICTORIA: I don't want to talk about this anymore. I'm so frustrated I want to scream.

   Your Turn

Write new sentences with the adjectives you underlined in Exercise 4. Read your sentences to a partner. Choose one of your partner's sentences to read to another group or the class.

SPOTLIGHT ON PARTICIPLES AS ADJECTIVES

Some movies **bore** the audience.

That movie was **boring.** = That movie bored (someone).

The audience was **bored.** = The audience was bored (by the movie).

The movie's special effects **amazed** us.

The special effects were **amazing.** = The special effects amazed (someone).

The audience was **amazed.** = The audience was amazed (by the special effects).

Participles used as adjectives describe nouns or pronouns.

Exercise 5: Complete the sentences with the correct adjective.

1. Emma told the other employees an (*interesting/interested*) _____ story about her family.

2. The ending of Emma's story was (*surprising/surprised*) _____.

3. Joe looked (*irritating/irritated*) _____ after he read his performance review.

4. No one was (*shocking/shocked*) _____ when Joe didn't go to the company picnic.

5. Sara got lost on her way to the picnic because of the (*confusing/confused*) _____ directions.

6. Jane went with some friends from work to a (*fascinating/fascinated*) _____ exhibit at the art museum.

7. Only one person thought the exhibit was (*disappointing/disappointed*) _____.

8. Jane thought that person was just too (*tiring/tired*) _____ to enjoy herself.

In Your Experience

Talk about the questions below in a group.
Then share your answers with another group or the class.

Do you think it's important to socialize with people from school or work? Why or why not? What social events do schools or companies have in your native country? Who attends? Is it important to attend? Why?

GET GRAPHIC

Read the bar graph below. The graph shows a Chicago family's entertainment expenses from last month.

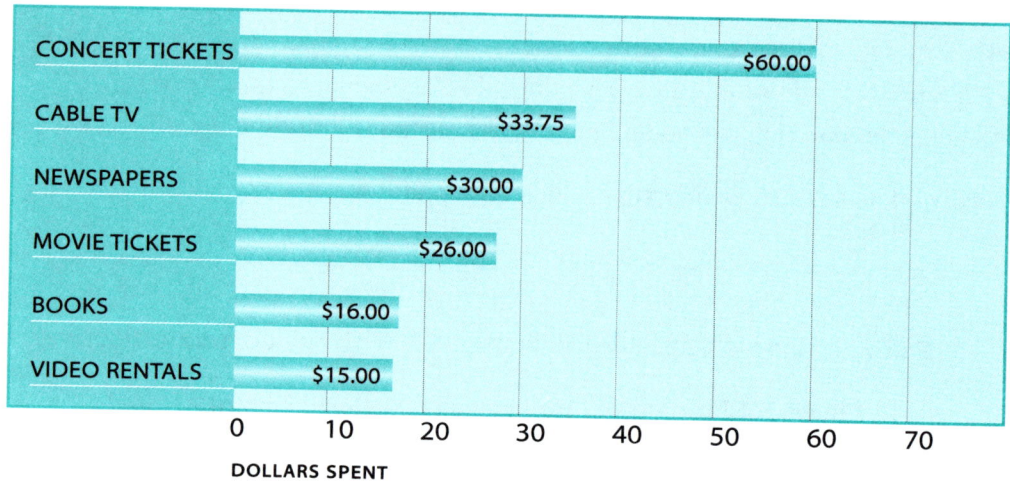

Exercise 6: Think about your family's entertainment expenses in an average month. Make a list of those expenses and the amount of money each one represents. Use the information to make your own entertainment bar graph. Then share your graph with a partner or group.

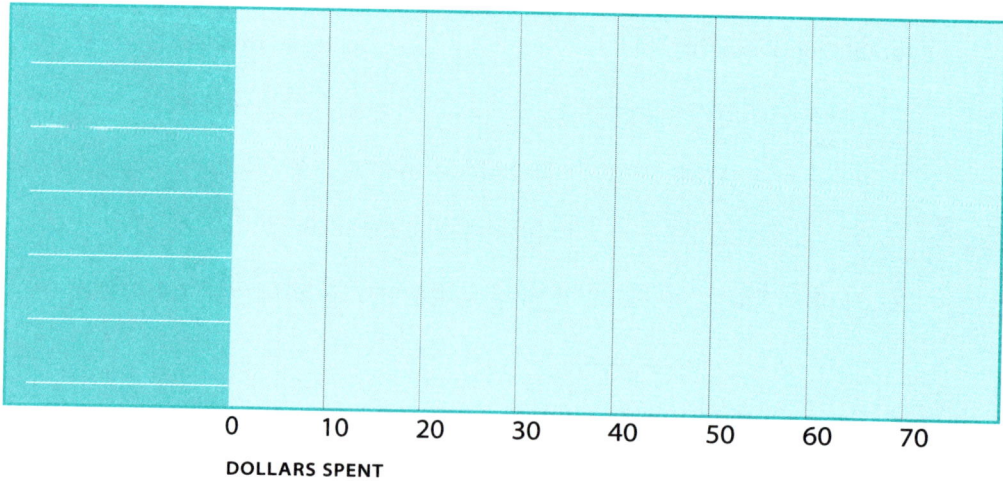

  In Your Experience

Discuss entertainment with the class. Ask questions like these:

What do you do for entertainment in the United States?

Did you do different things in your native country? Why?

Do you spend more or less money on entertainment in the United States than you did in your native country? Why?

What things do you do for entertainment that cost little or no money?

ISSUES AND ANSWERS

Read the letters about socializing at work. If you don't know the meaning of a word, use a dictionary or ask your teacher. Then write an answer to "Not Single."

Ask ABDUL and ANITA

DEAR ABDUL:

A co-worker invited everyone in my department to her house for a party. She asked us to bring food. In my country the host provides all the food and drinks. Is my co-worker cheap? When I told my husband about this, he was angry. He said we shouldn't go to the party because my co-worker insulted us. What do you think I should do?

INSULTED

DEAR INSULTED:

Believe it or not, many people in the United States ask guests to bring food to parties. They are not insulting anybody when they do this. It's just a different custom. Not going to the party may cause more problems for you in the future. We all have to do things we don't like that are necessary for our jobs.

ABDUL

DEAR ANITA:

My company is having a party at a hotel during the winter holidays. Husbands and wives are not invited. My wife thinks this is wrong, and she doesn't want me to attend the party. I have only worked at this company for a few months.

NOT SINGLE

DEAR NOT SINGLE:

_____

_____

_____

_____

_____

Exercise 7: Write your own letter to Abdul and Anita about a problem you have with socializing at work or at school. Ask a partner to respond to your letter. Share the letters and answers with another pair. Ask if they agree or disagree with the answers and why.

WRAP-UP

In pairs or groups make an idea map about why people need entertainment in their lives.

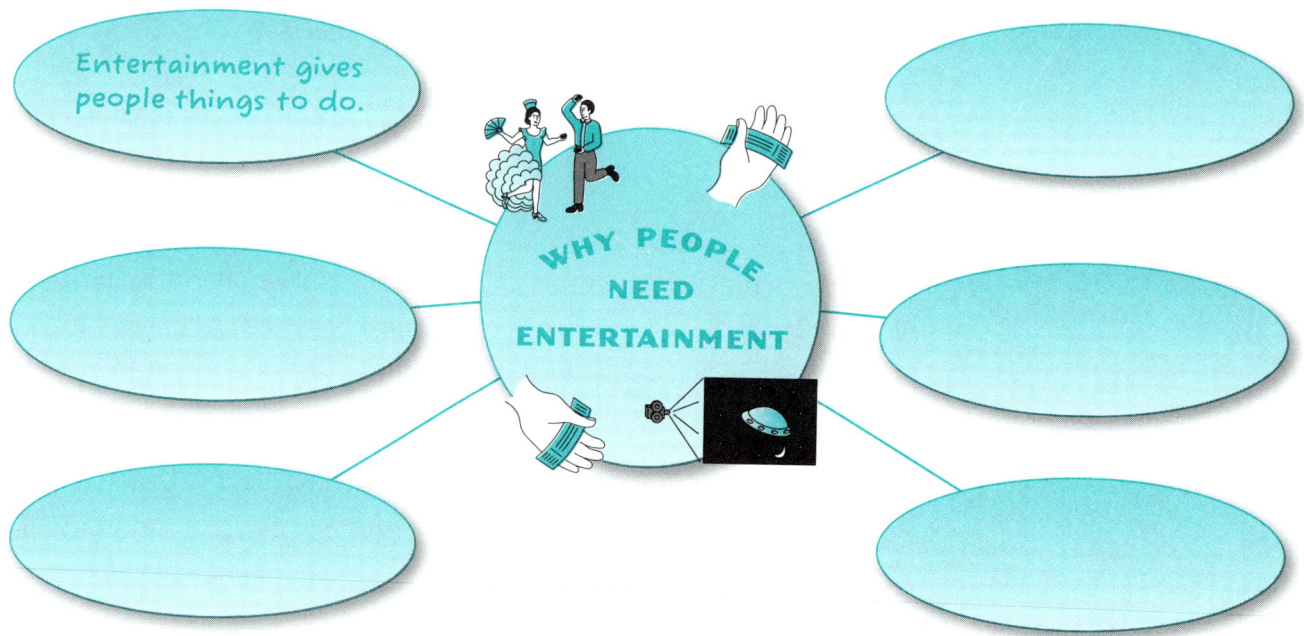

Entertainment gives people things to do.

WHY PEOPLE NEED ENTERTAINMENT

Share your ideas with the class.

Think About Learning

In this unit you learned a variety of skills and language structures. Look at the items below and check how easy or difficult each one was for you. At the bottom write one other thing you learned.

SKILLS / STRUCTURES	Page	easy ☺	so-so 😐	difficult ☹
Talk about people's problems	61			
Understand conversations about socializing at work	62			
Read a performance brochure	65			
Talk about dancing	66			
Make a bar graph	70			
Read and solve problems	67			
Use an idea map	72			
Use present participles as adjectives	63			
Use past participles as adjectives	68			
Choose the correct adjective	69			

Read the comic strip with a partner. Ask each other the questions below. Then share your answers with another pair or the class.

Andrew Lan is having trouble catching fish.

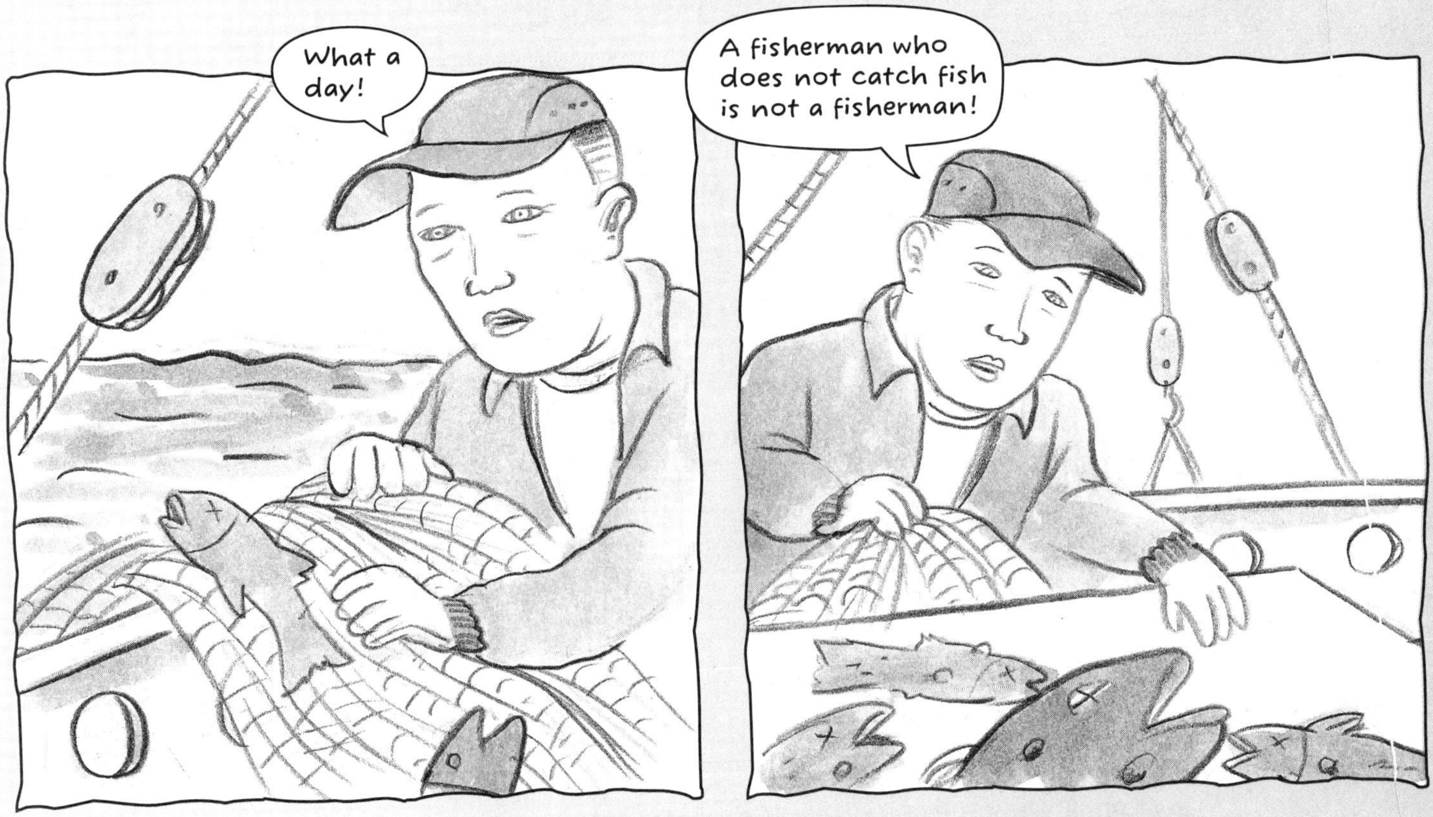

> What a day!

> A fisherman who does not catch fish is not a fisherman!

FACTS   What is this man's job? What's the problem?

FEELINGS   How does he feel?

AND YOU?   Have you ever felt bad about your job? Have you ever known people who could not do their jobs any more?

COMPARISONS   Are there problems like this in your country? Why or why not?

ACTIONS   What should this man do next?

Now write or tell the story in your own words.

SPOTLIGHT ON RELATIVE CLAUSES WITH *WHO*

I interviewed a fisherman. He was from Vietnam.
I interviewed a fisherman **who** was from Vietnam.

I talked to a woman. She was a reporter.
I talked to a woman **who** was a reporter.

She spoke to a fisherman. He was worried about dead fish.
She spoke to a fisherman **who** was worried about dead fish.

Relative clauses describe people or things.
They begin with the relative pronouns *who*, *which*, or *that*.
Use *who* to describe people.

Exercise 1: Read the sentences below. Combine each pair of sentences into one sentence. Use a relative clause with *who*.

1. Jack is a neighbor. He owns a boat.

   <u>Jack is a neighbor who owns a boat.</u>

2. I have a friend named Janet. She lives near a river.

   _____

3. You met my cousin. He goes white-water rafting every summer.

   _____

4. This is my co-worker. She likes to go fishing.

   _____

5. Meet my ESL teacher. She swims a mile every day.

   _____

Your Turn

Write three to five sentences about your classmates, neighbors, family, or co-workers. Use relative clauses with *who*. Share your sentences with the class.

Person to Person

Listen to these conversations. With a partner finish the last conversation. Use a relative clause with *who* if you can. Then practice the conversations with your partner.

KHALIL: Want to go white-water rafting this weekend?

KEN: Around here? Where?

KHALIL: In Wisconsin. It's just a three-hour drive from here.

KEN: Sure, I'd love to. How did you find out about this place?

KHALIL: I work with a man who went there last weekend. He had a lot of fun.

EMMA: You look happy and relaxed. What did you do over the weekend?

JUANA: I stayed on a houseboat on the Mississippi River.

EMMA: Isn't that expensive?

JUANA: Yeah, it is. But I didn't pay anything.

EMMA: You're kidding.

JUANA: No, I'm not. My sister has a friend who won a contest on the radio. The prize was a weekend on a houseboat.

PABLO: Do you know what you want to order yet?

MARIA: No. I love swordfish, but I refuse to eat it anymore.

PABLO: What are you talking about?

MARIA: The swordfish in the Mediterranean Sea and the Atlantic Ocean are almost gone. People who eat swordfish are helping to make them extinct!

SOON: I'm thirsty. Can I have a soda?

LEE: Why don't you have a glass of water? It's good for you.

SOON: I don't like water.

LEE: _____

Your Turn

Write a conversation about someone you know who did something interesting lately. Include a relative clause with *who*. Share your conversation with a group or the class. For example, write, "I have a co-worker who rides a bicycle 10 miles to work every day."

READING FOR REAL

When people visit certain parts of the United States, they often like to eat fish or other seafood from that area. In the Pacific Northwest, people eat salmon. Along the Mississippi River, they eat catfish. In Maryland and Virginia, they eat crab cakes.

Read the recipes for crab cakes and salmon steaks with mustard sauce.

Crab Cakes

INGREDIENTS:

1/4 cup chopped fresh parsley
3 tablespoons chopped green onions
1 pound crab meat
1/2 teaspoon salt
1/8 teaspoon black pepper
1 teaspoon dry mustard
1 egg, lightly beaten
1/2 cup fine breadcrumbs
1/2 cup butter

Combine the first seven ingredients. Shape into small round cakes about three inches across. Roll in bread crumbs. Cook about 10 minutes in butter until golden brown all over.

Makes 8–10 cakes/Serves 4–5

Salmon Steaks with Mustard Sauce

INGREDIENTS:

4 six-ounce salmon steaks
3 tablespoons fresh chopped dill
2 tablespoons low-fat mayonnaise
1 tablespoon white wine vinegar
2 teaspoons Dijon mustard
I teaspoon sugar
1/4 teaspoon salt/ground pepper

Preheat broiler. Grease rack in the broiling pan. Sprinkle salmon with 1/8 teaspoon salt and 1/8 teaspoon ground pepper. Broil salmon 10 minutes or until fish flakes easily. While salmon is cooking, prepare the sauce. In small bowl, mix the mayonnaise, vinegar, mustard, sugar, 2 tablespoons dill, and 1/8 teaspoon each salt and pepper. Serve with the salmon.

Serves four.

  Exercise 2: Fill in the chart below using the information from the recipes above.

	CRAB CAKES	SALMON	BOTH	NEITHER
Takes several hours to cook				
Is low in fat				
Serves four				
Cooks in the broiler				
Contains fresh fruit				

 ## Talk About It

With the class do a survey. Ask, "Have you ever eaten crab cakes or salmon? Where? When? Which recipe would you like to try?" Share your reasons.
How do you prepare fish? What kind of fish do you like?
Bring a favorite recipe to share with the class.

CULTURE CORNER

Look at the picture and read the paragraph below.

Water is essential for life. Some people think there will always be enough water for them to use and drink. However, many others think that isn't true, especially since so much water is polluted. The Environmental Protection Agency (EPA) says more than half of the rivers, lakes, and streams in the United States are polluted.

Your Turn

Talk about the questions below in a small group. Share the answers with another group or the class.

Do you worry about polluted water? Why or why not?

Does your native country have polluted water or other water problems? What are the problems?

Can you name any other countries with water problems? What are the countries? What are the problems?

What do you do to conserve, or save, water?

In Your Experience

Work with a partner. Look at the map below. Fill in as many names of the bodies of water as you can. Share your answers with another pair. If answers are still missing, look at a U.S. map to find them.

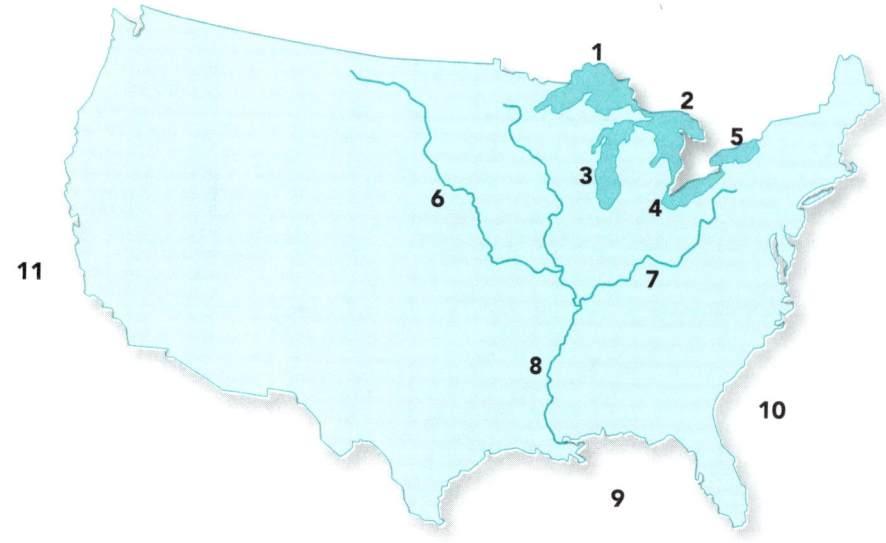

1. _____
2. _____
3. _____
4. _____
5. _____
6. _____
7. _____
8. _____
9. _____
10. _____
11. _____

SCENE 2

Read the comic strip with a partner. Ask each other the questions below.
Then share your answers with another pair or the class.

Andrew Lan has to sell his fishing boat.

FACTS	What's the problem? What happened to Andrew's boat?
FEELINGS	How does he feel?
AND YOU?	Have you ever felt like Andrew?
COMPARISONS	In your country do people have to change careers or jobs in midlife?
ACTIONS	What do you think Andrew will do next?

VOCABULARY PROMPTS

Before you listen, talk about these words in a group.

recently   subjects   accounting   make a living

SOUND BITES

While You Listen   Listen for answers to these questions. Take notes.

What kind of job is Andrew interested in?
Why isn't Andrew a fisherman anymore?

After You Listen   Discuss the answers to the questions with a group.

SPOTLIGHT ON RELATIVE CLAUSES WITH *WHICH* AND *THAT*

Use relative clauses with *which* and *that* to describe things.

Andrew wants a job **that** has a future.
He wants a job **which** pays well and **which** he enjoys.

When the information in the clause is necessary to identify the thing, either word can be used.

The personnel manager is in Office 10, **which** is down the hall.

When the information in the clause is not necessary, just additional, then *which* is used.

Andrew has a friend **that** works at the community college.
You can also use *that* to describe people, but *who* is preferred.

Exercise 3: Andrew is talking to Lukas, who is a job counselor at the community college. Read their conversation. Underline the relative clauses and circle the nouns they are describing.

LUKAS: Andrew, what kind of job are you interested in?

ANDREW: I don't know for sure yet. I had a (job) that I loved. I hope I can find another job that I like as much.

LUKAS: Tell me a little about the work that you did.

ANDREW: I've been a fisherman all my life. About five years ago, I bought my own boat, which I recently had to sell. I couldn't catch enough fish to pay the loan for the boat, feed my family, and pay my other bills!

LUKAS: Do you have any education or special skills that you want to tell me about?

ANDREW: I graduated from high school, and I've taken a few community college classes in subjects that interested me.

LUKAS: Oh, like what?

ANDREW: I took classes in biology, small business management, and accounting. They were things that also helped me do my job better.

LUKAS: Why aren't you a fisherman anymore?

ANDREW: Haven't you heard about all the fish that died in the waters around here? I couldn't catch enough healthy fish to sell. A lot of us who had just one or two boats couldn't make a living anymore.

  Your Turn

With a partner write your own interview with someone who is looking for a new career. Try to use relative clauses with *which* and *that*. Role-play your interview for another pair or the class.

SPOTLIGHT ON WORD ORDER IN RELATIVE CLAUSES

Andrew is a man. He likes working outdoors.
Andrew is a man **who likes working outdoors**.

Some of the fishermen were unemployed.
They couldn't sell their boats.
Some of the fishermen **who couldn't sell their boats** were unemployed.

Relative clauses can come in the middle or at the end of a sentence.
They always follow the words they are describing.

Exercise 4: Rewrite the sentences below in your notebook.
Combine each of the two sentences into one sentence with a relative clause.

1. Environmentalists believe there is a worldwide fish crisis.
   They study waters and fish.

   Environmentalists who study waters and fish believe there is a worldwide fish crisis.

2. Building too much and polluting are dangerous activities. They kill fish.

   _____

3. Fishermen catch bluefin tuna to sell to Japan. The tuna sell for as much as $80,000.

   _____

4. A fisherman can make a lot of money. He catches a bluefin tuna.

   _____

5. Consumers can stop overfishing. They refuse to buy endangered fish.

   _____

  Your Turn

Write three to five sentences about the kinds of fish that you eat regularly.
Read your sentences to a partner. Try to use relative clauses
with *who*, *which*, and *that*. For example, you could write,
"I eat tuna that is fresh."

GET GRAPHIC

In 1995 the world fishing industry caught 90 million tons of ocean fish. Eleven countries caught 58.2 million tons of fish. This was 65 percent of all the fish caught in the oceans. Here is a table that shows the eleven countries and the millions of tons of fish that they caught.

COUNTRY	FISH CAUGHT IN MILLIONS OF TONS	COUNTRY	FISH CAUGHT IN MILLIONS OF TONS
Chile	7.4	Peru	8.9
China	11.6	Russia	4.3
India	3.3	South Korea	2.3
Indonesia	3.5	Thailand	3.6
Japan	5.9	United States	5.2
Norway	2.5		

Exercise 5: Use the information from the table above to make a bar graph.

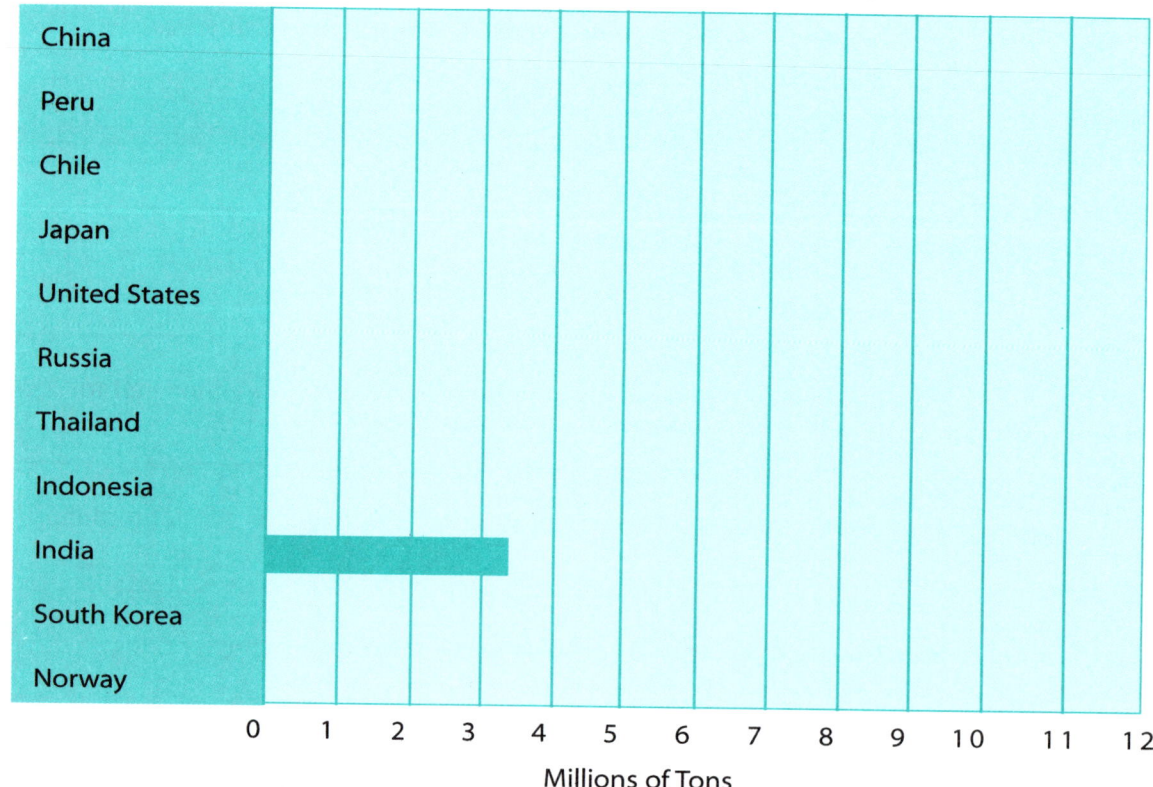

In Your Experience

Ask and answer the following questions in a small group.

Do you think the countries listed in the graph caught too much fish? Why?
Which is more important, protecting animals and the environment or feeding people?

ISSUES AND ANSWERS: LETTERS TO THE EDITOR

Many people read the reporter's interview with Andrew Lan, and they wrote letters to the newspaper. Read the letters. If you don't know the meaning of a word, use a dictionary or ask your teacher.

BOWIE—You recently published an interview with a fisherman, Andrew Lan, who was complaining about dead fish. I am tired of reading about people like him, who spoil the environment. There is no reason to have sympathy for him. He and others like him are ruining the world. We wouldn't have to worry about so many dead fish if people stopped eating them. I say eat vegetables!

A VEGETARIAN READER

CHESAPEAKE—I just read the letter from "A Vegetarian Reader" and I am furious. That person missed the point completely. The problem is not that Andrew Lan is a fish killer. He lost his job and his boat because big companies pollute our waters. We should be trying to stop pollution. More than 50 percent of the water in this country is polluted by farms and factories. We need to pass better laws to stop this. Meanwhile, I eat vegetables *and* fish!

SUE NICKOLS

Exercise 6: What is the main idea of each letter? Write the main ideas on the lines below and share them with a partner.

1. A Vegetarian Reader: _____

_____

_____

2. Sue Nickols: _____

_____

_____

Exercise 7: Talk about the questions below with a group or the class.

Which letter do you agree with? Why?

What sentences in the letters are opinions? Circle them.

What sentences are facts? Underline them.

Exercise 8: Write your own letter to a newspaper editor about water pollution, overfishing, or another topic that interests you. Share it with the class.

WRAP-UP

With a group make an idea map about ways to protect our waters.

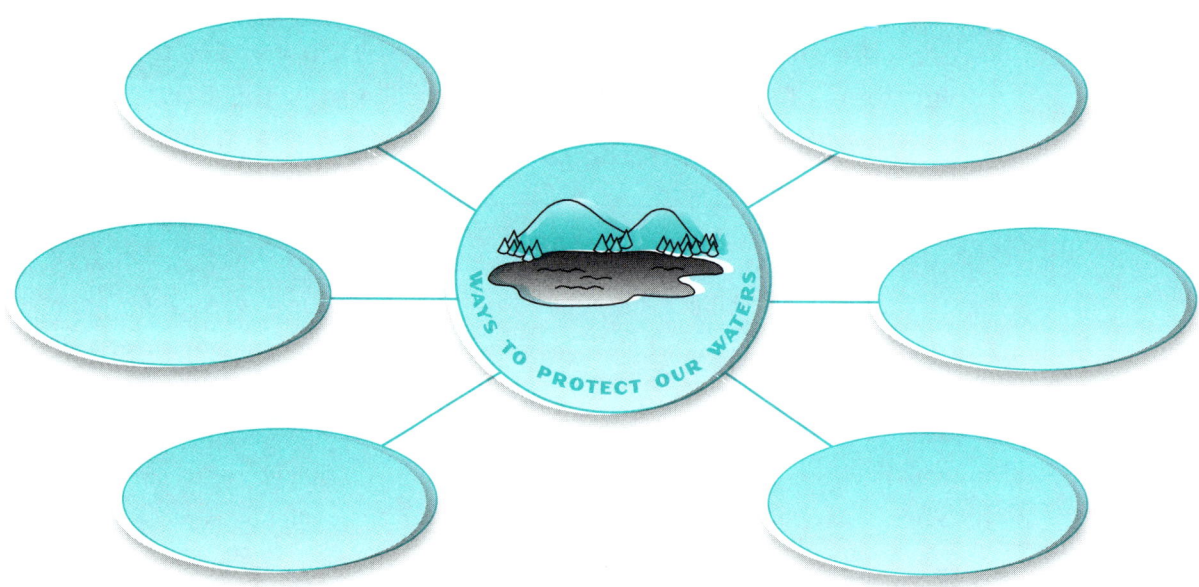

Present your ideas to another group or the class. Use relative clauses with *who*, *which*, and *that* when you talk about your ideas. For example, say, "People should stop buying fish that is endangered."

Think About Learning

In this unit you learned a variety of skills and language structures. Look at the items below and check how easy or difficult each one was for you. At the bottom write one other thing you learned.

SKILLS / STRUCTURES	Page	easy ☺	so-so ☺	difficult ☹
Talk about people's problems	73			
Understand recorded conversations	74			
Read a recipe	77			
Read a map	78			
Make a bar graph	82			
Discuss ways to conserve water	78			
Read and write letters to the editor	83			
Make an idea map	84			
Use relative clauses with *who*	75			
Use relative clauses with *which* and *that*	80			
Use correct word order in relative clauses	81			

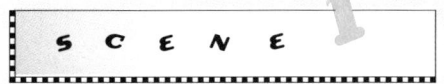

Read the comic strip with a partner. Ask each other the questions below.
Then share your answers with another pair or the class.

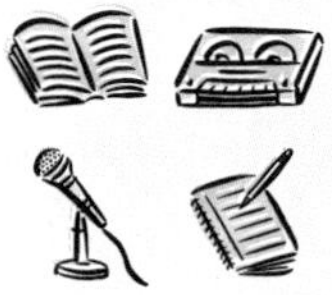

A Dream Up in Smoke . . .

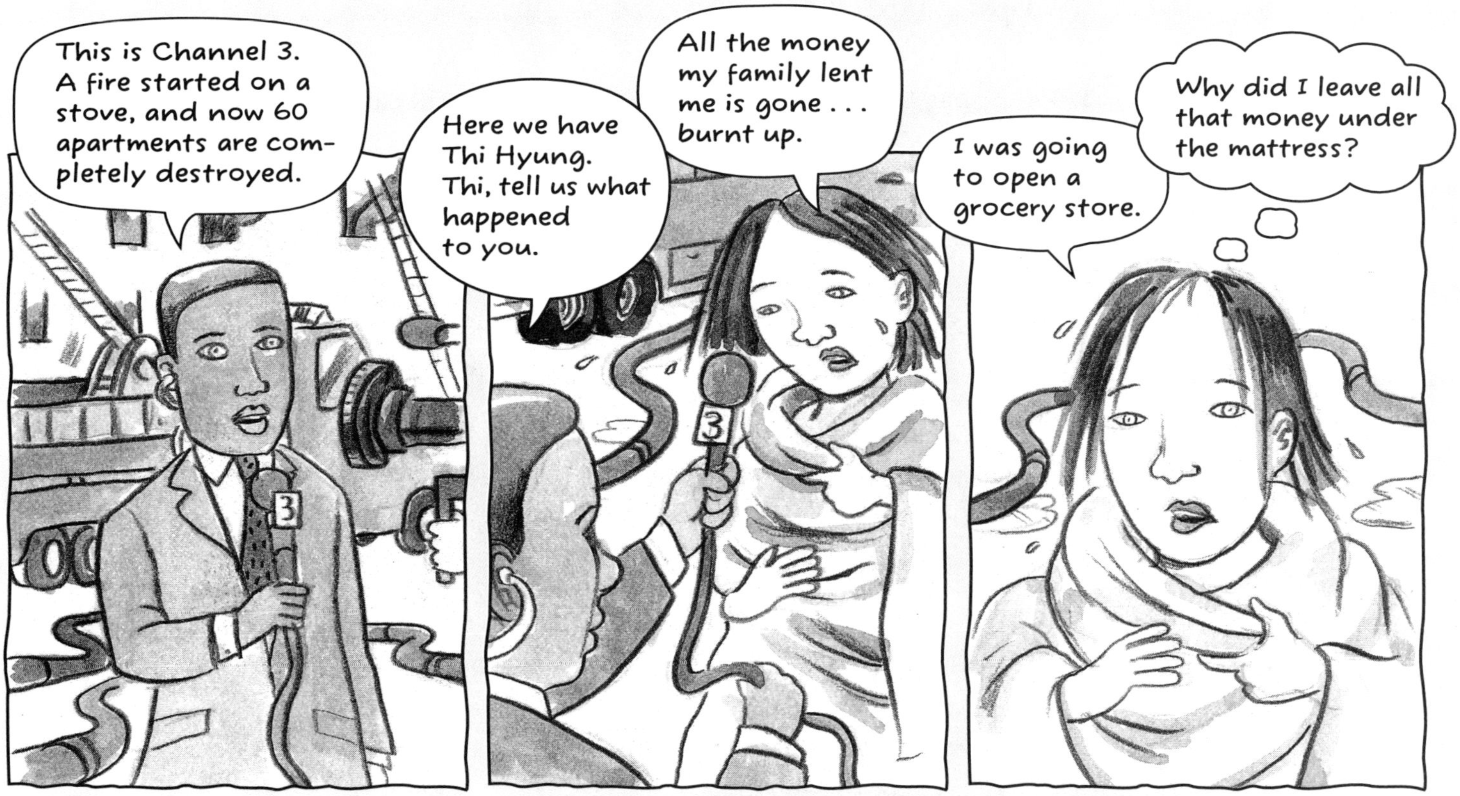

> This is Channel 3. A fire started on a stove, and now 60 apartments are completely destroyed.

> Here we have Thi Hyung. Thi, tell us what happened to you.

> All the money my family lent me is gone . . . burnt up.

> I was going to open a grocery store.

> Why did I leave all that money under the mattress?

FACTS	What's the problem?
FEELINGS	How does Thi feel?
AND YOU?	Has something like this ever happened to you?
COMPARISONS	Where do people in the United States put money they have saved? Explain how things are different or the same in your native country.
ACTIONS	What should Thi do? What do you think will happen next?

Now write or tell the story in your own words.

SOUND BITES

Listen to the six radio advertisements selling banking services.

Before You Listen In a group talk about the pictures and the meaning of the words below. If you need help, ask your teacher.

While You Listen Number the pictures from 2 through 6 as you listen.

_____ Home Equity Loans

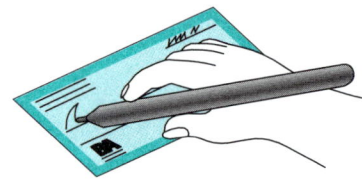

_____ Checking Accounts with Interest

1 Small Business Loans

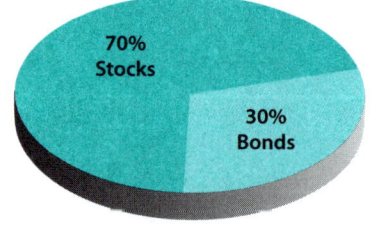

_____ Investment Funds for College

_____ Retirement Financial Planning

_____ Homeowner Loans

After You Listen Use the numbered pictures to talk about the advertisements with a partner. What other information did you hear?

Your Turn

With a group talk about which banking services you would or would not be interested in and why.

⚡ SPOTLIGHT ON DIRECT AND INDIRECT OBJECTS

She sent **the bill**.

The direct object answers the question *what* or *who* receives the action.

She sent **the bill**	**to him**.
(direct object)	(indirect object)

The indirect object answers the questions *to whom* or *for whom* the direct object is intended.

She sent **him**	**the bill**.
(indirect object)	(direct object)

Notice that the preposition *to* is dropped when the indirect object moves to the middle position.

Exercise 1: In the sentences below, underline the direct object and circle the indirect object. Then rewrite the sentence, moving the indirect object to the middle position. Don't forget to drop the preposition!

1. The owner of the company gave <u>a bonus</u> to (my whole department.)

   The owner of the company gave my whole department a bonus.

2. I need to send some money to my family.

   _____

3. I lent $5.00 to my friend John the other day.

   _____

4. You can save money for your family with these coupons.

   _____

Exercise 2: Unscramble the words to make sentences with direct and indirect objects. Write them in your notebook.

1. a / me / giving / noise / this / headache / is

2. questions / don't / boss / when / understand / ask / you / your

3. offered / after / me / job / interview / they / a / the /

4. payments / the / charges / I / late / me / bank / when / make

Person to Person

Listen to these conversations. With a partner finish the last conversation.
Then practice the conversations with your partner.

ALDO: The rent check bounced because we didn't have enough money in our account.

ROSA: Are you kidding?

ALDO: No, I'm not. And now the bank is charging us an overdraft fee.

ROSA: I told you we needed a monthly budget.

LUCIA: Didn't you lend Ibrahim 20 dollars last week?

CHRIS: Yeah, he needed to pay an application fee.

LUCIA: Did he pay you back yet?

CHRIS: No, but I owe him 75 dollars from last week!

JEN: How was your interview?

PING: Pretty good, but they asked me lots of hard questions

JEN: So did they offer you the job?

PING: They're going to call me next week.

JOE: I can't pay all my bills.

STEVE: Do you want to save your family some money?

JOE: Sure, how?

STEVE: _____

Your Turn

With a partner write a conversation about saving money. Use direct and indirect objects with verbs such as *pay*, *owe*, and *save*. Share your conversation with a group or the class.

In small groups talk about the words below.

home equity loans   cash value   life insurance   priorities

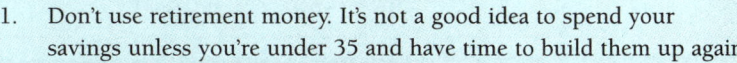

READING FOR REAL

Read the article below about starting a small business.

STARTING A SMALL BUSINESS ON A SMALL BUDGET

Many people are afraid to start their own businesses. Five out of six small businesses fail during the first five years of operation. How can you get the money you need to start a business? Here are six tips to remember.

1. Don't use retirement money. It's not a good idea to spend your savings unless you're under 35 and have time to build them up again.

2. Don't take out home equity loans. You don't want large monthly payments in addition to all your other expenses.

3. Use credit cards. Although interest rates are high, most credit card companies will allow you to make minimum, low monthly payments.

4. Borrow against the cash value of life insurance policies. Find out how much you can borrow. What will happen to the value of your insurance? Can you borrow money and not pay it back?

5. Decide how you want to pay back friends and family. Should you give them back the money you borrowed? Or should you make them partners in the business? If you make people partners, you have to be sure that you can really work with them.

6. Make a business plan. Set your goals and stick to them. Make a list of priorities and keep them in mind in the years ahead.

Exercise 3: In groups circle T *(true)* or F *(false)* after each statement. Discuss your answers. For each false statement circle the correct information in the article.

1. Most small businesses fail before they are five years old.	T	F
2. It's OK to use retirement money if you're over 55.	T	F
3. Large home equity loans are a good way to get cash.	T	F
4. Never make friends and family your business partners.	T	F
5. Change your plans and goals from time to time.	T	F

Talk About It

With a partner ask and answer the questions below.

Do you want to own your own business? If so, what kind?

What is good or bad about having your own business?

CULTURE CORNER

In a group talk about the meaning of the words in the chart below.
If you need help, use a dictionary or ask your teacher.

Exercise 4: Fill out the chart for yourself. Which benefits do you have?
Use check marks.

COMMON EMPLOYEE BENEFITS

Benefit	I have this benefit	I don't have this benefit	I don't know
Vacation			
Sick pay			
Health insurance			
Dental insurance			
Life insurance			
Disability insurance			
Pension			
401(k) or 403(b) plan			
Profit sharing or stock purchase plan			
Financial help for family care			
Educational reimbursement			
Personal improvement programs			
Charitable donations			

Exercise 5: Talk about the chart with your group. Ask others about benefits
that are new to you. Who can you talk to at your workplace to find out about
your benefits?

Your Turn

Some of the benefits above relate to retirement. Circle the retirement benefits in
the chart. In groups make a list of other ways people can pay for their retirement.

_____

_____

_____

In Your Experience

How long do you plan to work? What will you do when you retire? Where will you live?
What worries or concerns do you have? Write a paragraph to share with the class.

Read the comic strip with a partner. Ask each other the questions below. Then share your answers with another pair or the class.

Thi is talking with her friend Rhoun several days after the fire.

FACTS	What are Thi and Rhoun talking about?
FEELINGS	What does Rhoun think? How does Thi feel?
AND YOU?	How do you feel about banks?
COMPARISONS	Do many people start small businesses in your native country? Is it easier or more difficult than in the United States?
ACTIONS	What do you think Thi should do?

VOCABULARY PROMPTS

In a small group talk about the words below.

account   service charge   option   direct deposit

SOUND BITES

While You Listen Listen for answers to the questions below. Take notes. What kind of account does Thi want to open? What is direct deposit? What can Thi do with an ATM card? Who is Thi going to talk to next?

After You Listen Discuss the answers to the questions with a group.

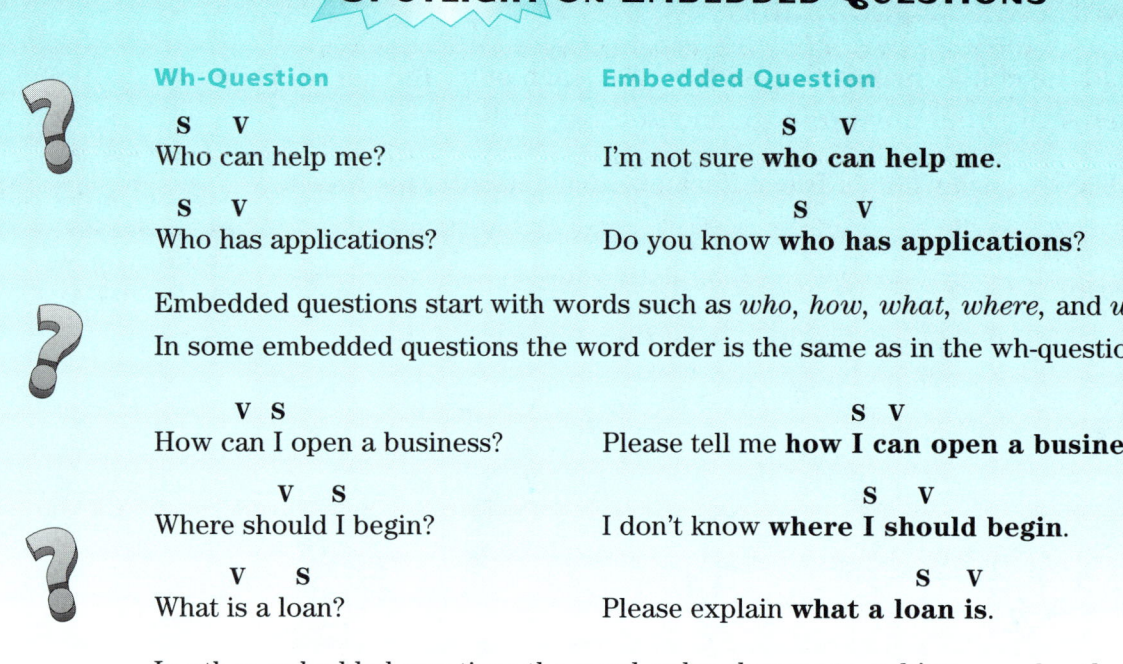

SPOTLIGHT ON EMBEDDED QUESTIONS

Wh-Question	Embedded Question
S V	**S V**
Who can help me?	I'm not sure **who can help me**.
S V	**S V**
Who has applications?	Do you know **who has applications**?

Embedded questions start with words such as *who, how, what, where,* and *when.*
In some embedded questions the word order is the same as in the wh-question.

V S	**S V**
How can I open a business?	Please tell me **how I can open a business**.
V S	**S V**
Where should I begin?	I don't know **where I should begin**.
V S	**S V**
What is a loan?	Please explain **what a loan is**.

In other embedded questions the word order changes to *subject + verb* order.

Exercise 6: Change the *wh-* questions into embedded questions.
First label the subject and verb in the question. Decide if the word order
will change. Write your answer and then label the subject and verb.
With a partner compare your answers.

>   V S
> 1. How can I open an account?
>
>   S   V
> Can you tell me ___how I can open an account?___ .
>
> 2. Which bank should I go to?
>
> I'm not sure _____ .
>
> 3. What happened to my application?
>
> Do you know _____ .
>
> 4. Where can I get an application?
>
> I need to know _____ .
>
> 5. What is my balance?
>
> Please tell me _____ .

  Your Turn

In small groups think of some questions that you would like to ask at a bank.
Use embedded questions with "Can you tell me . . . ?"

SPOTLIGHT ON MORE EMBEDDED QUESTIONS:
YES/NO QUESTIONS AND INFINITIVES

Yes/No Question	Embedded Question
Do I have enough money?	I don't know **whether I have enough money.**
Did I save enough?	I wonder **if I saved enough.**

Yes/No questions use *whether* or *if* in the embedded question. Note that helping verbs such as *do* and *did* are not used in the embedded question.

Please tell me **how I can open a business.**
Please tell me **how to open a business.**

I don't know **where I should begin.**
I don't know **where to begin.**

You can also use an infinitive—the *to* form of the verb—when the meaning of the embedded question is ability or necessity.

In questions, the word order is *wh-* + verb + subject
In embedded questions, the word order is *wh-* + subject + verb.

Exercise 7: Change these questions into embedded questions.
Rewrite the sentence two ways: with *can* or *should* and with infinitives.
Compare your answers with a partner.

1. Who should I write the check to?

   Do you know <u>who I should write the check to?</u>

   Do you know <u>who to write the check to?</u>

2. Should I invest money in the stock market?

   I'm not sure _____

   I'm not sure _____

3. Where can I get more information?

   I'd like to know _____

   I'd like to know _____

Your Turn

Money decisions can be very difficult. In groups think of yes/no questions about money. Change the questions into embedded questions using "I'm not sure . . ." and "I don't know whether . . ." Share your embedded questions with the class.

GET GRAPHIC

Look at the two graphs. Someone's savings rate is the part of that person's income that he or she saved instead of spending. The graph on the left shows savings rates in the United States. The graph on the right compares savings rates in the United States with rates in four other countries.

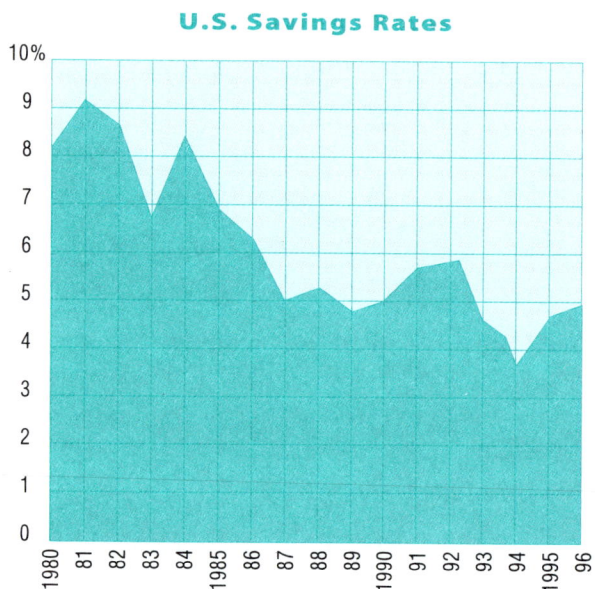

U.S. Savings Rates

United States and Other Countries

Exercise 8: Use the information in the graphs to complete the paragraphs below.

People in the United States don't save as much money as they used to.

In 1981 the savings rate was a little more than _____ percent. In 1994 it was

less than _____ percent. From 1994 to 1996 the savings rate went _____.

On this graph the best three years for savings in the United States were _____,

_____, and _____.

In the United States the personal savings rate in 1996 was _____ percent.

It was _____ than the rates in Germany, Great Britain, Canada, and Japan.

The savings rate in Japan was _____ percent. This was _____ percent higher

than the rate in the United States.

In Your Experience

Do a survey. Ask these questions in small groups.
How many people save money out of every paycheck?
How many people have savings accounts or investments?
Use each group's information to make a graph for the class.

ISSUES AND ANSWERS

Read the letters below. If you don't know the meaning of a word, use a dictionary or ask your teacher. Write an answer to "Thinking About Retirement."

Ask MS. MONEY

DEAR MS. MONEY:

I just started a new job. My employer gave me a lot of forms to fill out, but I didn't understand all of them. One was for a 401(k) account. What is that? I didn't sign up because I don't know what it is. Did I make a mistake?

CONFUSED

DEAR CONFUSED:

You shouldn't sign things you don't understand, but a 401(k) is a good thing. This is a way for you to save for your retirement. Money is deducted from your paycheck before taxes. The company often adds additional money to your 401(k) account. This is a good way to supplement your retirement income. Put as much money as you can in your 401(k).

MS. MONEY

DEAR MS. MONEY:

I'm a 35-year-old unmarried woman. I'm worried about retirement. I don't know how much money I am going to need. How can I find out what to do to plan for my future?

THINKING ABOUT RETIREMENT

DEAR THINKING:

_____

_____

_____

_____

_____

Exercise 9: Now write your own letter asking for financial advice. Your partner will answer the letter. Then present your letter and answer to the class.

Dear _____:

_____

_____

_____

Dear _____:

_____

_____

_____

WRAP-UP

With a group make a T-chart about how you spend your money.
Answer these questions. Which of your expenses are fixed, or stay the
same every month? Which of your expenses are flexible, or change?

FIXED EXPENSES	FLEXIBLE EXPENSES
Rent or Mortgage	Groceries

Show your T-chart to another group. Compare your charts. How are they the same?
How are they different? Ask and answer questions about your charts.
Use direct and indirect objects and embedded questions if you can.

Think About Learning

In this unit you learned a variety of skills and language structures.
Look at the items below and check how easy or difficult each
one was for you. At the bottom write one other thing you learned.

SKILLS / STRUCTURES	Page	easy ☺	so-so 😐	difficult ☹
Talk about people's problems	85			
Understand bank advertisements	86			
Read tips for starting a business	89			
Talk about benefits	90			
Read a bar graph and a line graph	94			
Read and solve problems	95			
Use a T-chart to present ideas	96			
Use direct and indirect objects	87			
Use embedded questions	92, 93			

UNIT 9

GETTING HELP IN YOUR COMMUNITY

Read the comic strip with a partner. Ask each other the questions below.
Then share your answers with another pair or the class.

Celia's two-year-old son Miguel is getting into trouble.

FACTS	What's the problem? What happened?
FEELINGS	How does Celia feel? Why?
AND YOU?	Do you know anyone who has raised children? What are some of the difficulties with small children?
COMPARISONS	What do families in your native country do in situations like this?
ACTIONS	What should Celia do? What do you think will happen next?

Now write or tell the story in your own words.

VOCABULARY PROMPTS

In small groups talk about the words below.

battered   hotline   prenatal   substance   abuse   youth

SOUND BITES

Before You Listen In some countries people ask only their family or close friends for help with personal problems. In the United States there are also *community resource centers* where people can get help. Look at the Community Resource Center Directory below and discuss the meaning of each service with your teacher.

While You Listen Listen to eight people talk about themselves. Decide which service each one needs and write down the extension number.

COMMUNITY RESOURCE CENTER DIRECTORY

Service	Extension	Service	Extension
Battered women's shelter	321	Parenting classes	326
Child abuse hotline	322	Prenatal clinic	327
Depression hotline	323	Substance abuse hotline	328
Fair housing office	324	Translations / interpreters	329
Help for the elderly	325	Youth services	330

1. Celia   ext: __326__   5. Connie   ext: _____
2. Michael ext: _____   6. Ursula   ext: _____
3. Andrea   ext: _____   7. Kishor   ext: _____
4. Alex   ext: _____   8. Mark   ext: _____

After You Listen With a partner discuss why you chose each extension number.

Your Turn

In small groups make a list of the resources available to help people in your community. Which resources would be especially helpful to people you know? Discuss this question in groups.

SPOTLIGHT ON TIME CLAUSES

The manager seemed very friendly **while he was talking on the phone.**

    (main clause)   (time clause)

As soon as we walked into the office, things changed.

    (time clause)   (main clause)

Time clauses describe the main clause. Time clauses answer the question *When?*
When the time clause comes first, use a comma.

Before we met the manager, we were excited about the apartment.

We were feeling very positive **until we met him.**

When we walked into his office, he didn't seem friendly anymore.

We haven't returned to that building **since we went there that day.**

Exercise 1: Read the passage below. With a partner fill in the blanks
with the correct time expression from the grammar box above.
In some cases there are several correct answers.

I was never a good student. Since the very first day of kindergarten, I never liked school.

(1)_____ I was 15 years old, I decided to drop out.

Last year, my own son started having problems in school. His grades were

dropping, but (2) _____ I asked him about it, he refused to talk to me.

Then I had a meeting with Ms. Carlson. (3)_____ I met her, I thought

that she was probably like all the other teachers I knew. But (4)_____ she

walked in the door, I saw that she was different. (5)_____ I was talking

to her, I saw that she really cared.

(6)_____ I talked to Ms. Carlson, I went home feeling much better.

I could do something to help my son. I started asking to see my son's homework

and trying to help him. We also got into a study group.

Things are much better now. My advice to other parents is this: Don't wait

(7)_____ your kid drops out of school. Get involved now.

Your Turn

Think about your experiences in school. Was school easy or difficult?
Write sentences using time clauses and share them with a group.

Person to Person

Listen to these conversations. With a partner finish the last conversation.
Then practice the conversations with your partner.

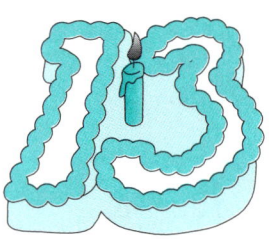

PATTI: What's wrong?

ELSA: Whenever I tell my kids to do something, they do just the opposite.

PATTI: I know. As soon as my daughter had her 13th birthday, she started fighting with me.

ELSA: I think all teenagers are like that!

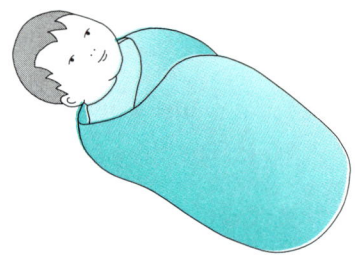

DR. LI: Before you deliver your baby, you should take a Lamaze class.

SUE: That's where you learn all the breathing techniques, right?

DR. LI: Yes, and while you're in the hospital, you'll be given information on child care.

SUE: Great! I want to learn as much as I can before the baby comes.

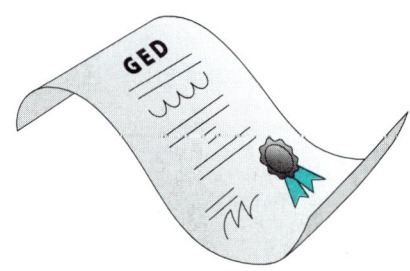

BOB: What are you going to do after you get your GED certificate?

KAY: I don't know, but I want to get a better job soon.

BOB: Well, as soon as I get my GED, I'm going to take a computer class at the community college.

KAY: That's a good idea.

MONA: Who's going to take care of the baby when you go back to work?

ZARA: I am. I'm going to work at the daycare center, so she can stay with me while I'm working.

MONA: _____

ZARA: _____

Your Turn

With a partner write a conversation about someone asking for help in the community.
Use time clauses wherever you can. Share your conversation with a group or the class.

In small groups talk about the words below.

hands-on   graduate   undergraduate   credit   noncredit

READING FOR REAL

Read the information Celia received about a community college.

CLASSES OFFERED AT PARKVIEW COMMUNITY COLLEGE

CMP375 CS/Introduction to Computers (1 cr)

In this hands-on course, students will learn the basics of computers.
Instructor Lena Stevens, M.A., is an expert in computer science.

COM523 CM/Communication and Relationships (0.5cr)

Students will learn all about communication in family and other relationships.
Instructor Luz Martinez, M.A., has 15 years of teaching experience and is director of the Multicultural Club.

How to Register	**Costs**
By Phone (602) 555-3399	Academic Credit
Register with credit card, 24 hours a day. Include course information, name, address, telephone number.	Graduate: $149 per credit hour
	Undergraduate: $99 per credit hour
BY MAIL	NONCREDIT
Continuing Education Department	$65 per day
Hawthorne Community College	$45 per day for senior citizens
200 Adams Street	Books are additional
Hawthorne, IN 70296	
	Questions? Call (800) 555-3399

Exercise 2: In small groups read the sentences and write *true* or *false* below.

1. Classes will take place at Hawthorne College. _____*false*_____

2. The communication and relationships class is five credits. _____

3. You can call or send in an application to register. _____

4. Undergraduate courses are less expensive than graduate courses. _____

5. Books are included in the registration fees. _____

Your Turn

Which course would you like to take? Is there another subject you would like to study? Discuss these questions with your group and explain your reasons.

VOCABULARY PROMPTS

In small groups talk about the words below.

time-out   get pushed over the edge   whine   can't stand

CULTURE CORNER

Read the article. In groups, discuss the questions below.

WHEN PARENTS NEED A TIME-OUT

Even the most patient parent can lose control. We do things we don't mean to and wonder how we let ourselves get pushed over the edge. Here are five strategies to help with those difficult situations.

1. **Problem:** Your child is whining, and you can't stand it.

   Strategy: Pay no attention to the whining or sit somewhere with the child until the whining stops. Then continue your activities with no more discussion.

2. **Problem:** Your kids interrupt when you're talking on the phone.

   Strategy: Explain that interrupting is not acceptable and suggest an activity for the child to do until your call is finished. Or call back later and make calls when the kids are asleep.

3. **Problem:** Your kids don't listen to you when you talk to them.

   Strategy: Make kids understand that if they do not do what you're asking, something will happen. If you say that they will not be able to watch TV, then unplug the TV. Kids will understand that you are serious.

4. **Problem:** When your kids fight, you start fighting too.

   Strategy: Don't take sides. Give a punishment to both kids. (Another mother says, "Make them hold hands for 10 minutes.") If the fight happens in the car, stop the car until the fighting stops.

5. **Problem:** Your kids lie to you, so you feel you can't trust them.

   Strategy: Let your child know that you are upset and why. Give a warning and a reasonable punishment. If necessary, get professional help. The lying might be a sign of a serious problem.

Your Turn

Talk about the article. Answer the questions.

What should parents do when their kids make them angry?
When and how should parents punish their children?

In Your Experience

Do you agree with the advice given in the article? In small groups discuss whether or not you agree. Share strategies from your own experience or culture.

Read the comic strip with a partner. Ask each other the questions below.
Then share your answers with another pair or the class.

Celia is in a parent support group at the Community Resource Center.

FACTS	What are the people in the group talking about?
FEELINGS	How does Celia feel? Why?
AND YOU?	Have you ever felt like that?
COMPARISONS	Do people in your native country have problems like Celia's? What do they do?
ACTIONS	What do you think Celia should do?

VOCABULARY PROMPTS

In a small group talk about the words below.

cool off   neat   fight over

SOUND BITES

While You Listen Listen for the answers to the questions below. Take notes.
What happened the other day? How does Celia feel? Why?

After You Listen Discuss the answers to the questions with a group.

SPOTLIGHT ON CLAUSES OF CAUSE AND EFFECT

I smoke.   My parents smoked.

I smoke **because my parents smoked.**

(effect)   (cause)

You can use *because* and *since* to combine
two separate sentences.

They smoked.   I thought it was OK.

Since they smoked, I thought it was OK.

        (cause)   (effect)

Because and *since* always begin the "cause" part of the sentence.
Since, *as*, and *now that* can also mean "because."

Exercise 3: With a partner match Column A with Column B.
Write the letter on the line.

COLUMN A

1. Now that there's a dental
   clinic at the center, _____ *e*

2. We called 911 _____

3. Gloria decided to look at the
   community center _____

4. Some young kids fight and
   play aggressively _____

5. Why don't you bring your
   kids to the pool _____

COLUMN B

a. as she had nothing better to do.

b. since there's no charge from
   9:00 A.M. to noon?

c. because it was an emergency.

d. because they see so much
   violence on TV.

e. I think I'll make an appointment
   to have my teeth cleaned.

  In Your Experience

What problems are there in your community (for example, gangs, crime, drugs)?
In groups make a list. Then discuss why you think these problems started.
Use *because* and *since*. With the class write your ideas on the board.

SPOTLIGHT ON CLAUSES OF OPPOSITION

Should there be handguns in the community?

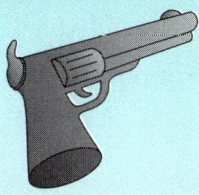 

Some people are for handguns, **while other people are against them.**

(opposition clause)

Although handguns can help protect you, they can also kill innocent people.

(opposition clause)

Some states have strict gun laws, **whereas other states don't.**

(opposition clause)

Clauses of opposition are used to contrast ideas, like the word *but*. The opposition clause can come at the beginning or the end of the sentence. You can use *while, whereas, though, although,* and *even though* to begin a clause of opposition.

Exercise 4: With a partner, match Column A with Column B. Write the letter on the line.

COLUMN A

1. Playing imaginative games helps develop kids' minds, _____

2. Playing outdoors makes kids healthy and strong, _____

3. Even though you might want to scream at your child, _____

4. Though educational TV has much to offer, _____

5. Fast food is convenient and fun for kids to eat, _____

COLUMN B

a. it is better to have a "time out" so you can both get control.

b. whereas staying inside can make them lazy.

c. although it usually isn't very healthy.

d. while watching TV can dull their imaginations.

e. there is no substitute for reading a book to a child.

Your Turn

In small groups choose one of the topics above—handguns or raising children—and have a discussion. Think of ideas that have two sides—*for* and *against*. Then, with the group, write sentences using *while, whereas, though, although,* and *even though.* Share your work with the class.

GET GRAPHIC

At last count, there were 12 million single parents in the United States. A single parent is a mother or father raising children alone. After a divorce many single mothers in particular have problems because of "deadbeat" fathers who don't pay the child-support money they are supposed to.

Look at the pie charts below.

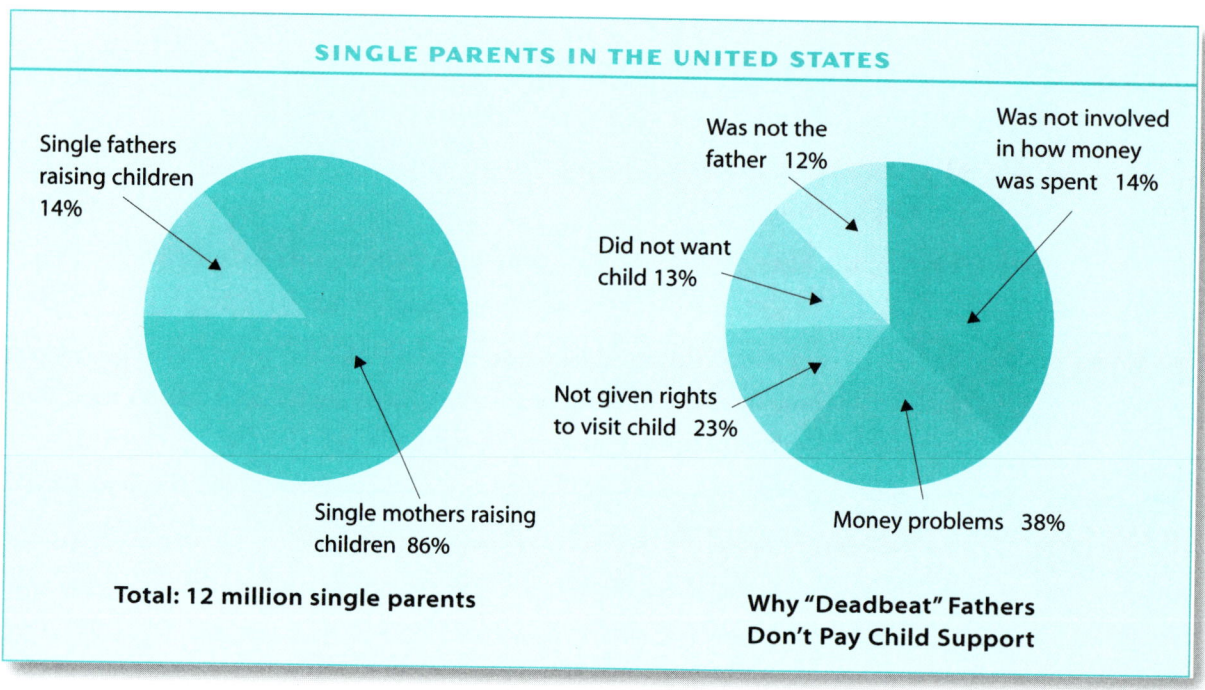

SINGLE PARENTS IN THE UNITED STATES

Single fathers raising children 14%

Single mothers raising children 86%

Total: 12 million single parents

Was not the father 12%

Was not involved in how money was spent 14%

Did not want child 13%

Not given rights to visit child 23%

Money problems 38%

Why "Deadbeat" Fathers Don't Pay Child Support

Exercise 5: In groups of two or three, write *true* or *false* after each statement below.

1. There are more than six times as many single mothers raising children as there are single fathers in the United States. ___*true*___

2. The pie chart on the left explains why there are more single mothers. _____

3. Twelve million fathers did not pay child support. _____

4. Money problems are a more important factor than rights to visit the child. _____

5. One quarter of the "deadbeats" did not pay child support because they either did not want the children or were not the fathers. _____

In Your Experience

In the same groups of two or three, talk about single parenting.

What are the difficulties single parents face?

What, if any, are the effects on the children?

What can be done about "deadbeat" parents?

ISSUES AND ANSWERS

Problems between people can exist in the workplace too. Read the company newsletter below. Write a response to the last question. Then write your own question and have a partner respond. Use clauses of cause and effect where possible.

TOOL MASTER WEEKLY NEWSLETTER

Got a question? We'll try to answer it.
This week we had a number of questions about
sexual harassment.

Question: *What is sexual harassment?*

Answer: Unwelcome sexual advances, requests for sexual favors, and other talking or touching of a sexual nature that affects your performance on the job.

Question: *Can men be harassed as well as women?*

Answer: The victim as well as the harasser can be a woman or a man. The victim does not have to be of the opposite sex.

Question: *What should I do if I think I'm being sexually harassed?*

Answer: Tell the harasser that the behavior is unwelcome and must stop. If it doesn't stop, contact the U.S. Equal Opportunity Commission in your local phone book or call (800) 669-EEOC.

Question: *I'm a man, and my boss is a woman. She keeps asking me to go out for a drink even though I'm married. I'm really uncomfortable. Is this sexual harassment? What suggestions do you have?*

Answer: _____

_____

_____

Question: _____

_____

_____

Answer: _____

_____

WRAP-UP

With the class or in groups, use an idea map like the one below to think of solutions to Jerzy's problems. Where can he get help? Share your ideas with the class.

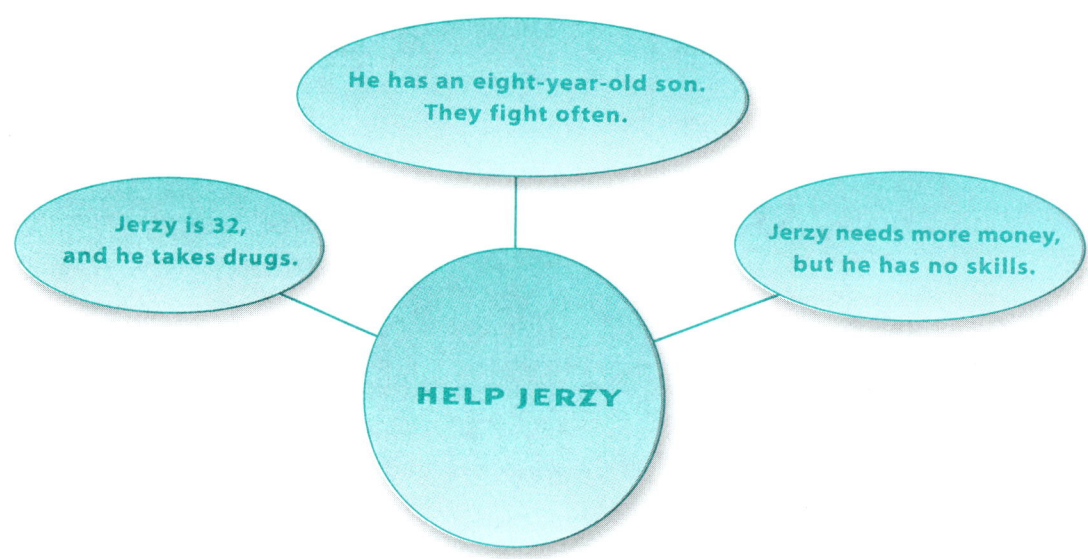

He has an eight-year-old son. They fight often.

Jerzy is 32, and he takes drugs.

Jerzy needs more money, but he has no skills.

HELP JERZY

Now, in small groups write a letter of advice to Jerzy.

Think About Learning

In this unit you learned a variety of skills and language structures. Look at the items below and check how easy or difficult each one was for you. At the bottom write one other thing you learned.

SKILLS / STRUCTURES	Page	easy ☺	so-so 😐	difficult ☹
Talk about people's problems	97, 103			
Understand conversations about problems	98			
Understand community resources	100			
Read a college brochure	101			
Understand parenting advice	102			
Read pie charts	106			
Read and write about sexual harassment	107			
Write a letter of advice	108			
Use time clauses	99			
Use clauses of cause and effect	104			
Use clauses of opposition	105			

MACHINES FOR COMMUNICATION

SCENE 1

Read the comic strip with a partner. Ask each other the questions below. Then share your answers with another pair or the class.

Roberto is opening his mail.

You have reached the Call On Us Phone Company. If you have a question about your bill press 1.

If my son is responsible for this bill, he'll never use the phone again!

FACTS	What's the problem? What happened to Roberto?
FEELINGS	How does he feel? How can you tell?
AND YOU?	Has this ever happened to you?
COMPARISONS	Would this be a problem in your native country?
ACTIONS	What should he do next?

Now write or tell the story in your own words.

VOCABULARY PROMPTS

In a small group talk about these words and write a sentence for each one.

otherwise   area   ASAP   gate   baggage claim

SOUND BITES

Before You Listen Share the sentences you wrote for the Vocabulary Prompts with the class. Then read the beginning of each sentence in Exercise 1 below.

While You Listen In your notebook take notes on the answering machine messages.

After You Listen Compare your notes with a partner. Did you write the same information?

Exercise 1: Complete the sentences using the notes you took for the Sound Bites.

1. If you need to speak to Joe, *he'll be home after 8:00 P.M.*

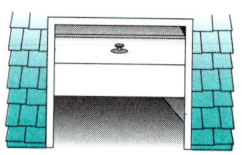

2. If Mrs. Lopez can wait, Joe'll _____ _____ .

3. If you leave your name and number, they'll _____ .

4. If she's late, she'll _____ _____ .

5. If parents want their child's homework assignment, they'll have to _____ _____ .

6. If you want to talk to Jon, you'll have to _____ _____ .

Your Turn

Now write a message to record for your own answering machine.
Read it to a group or the class.

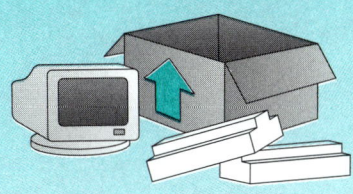

SPOTLIGHT ON CONDITIONAL WITH WILL

Action

If you buy a new computer,
(first event)

Possible Consequence

you'll have to learn new software.
(second event)

Possible Consequence

You'll have to learn new software
(second event)

Action

if you buy a new computer.
(first event)

Use future conditional to talk about things that may happen in the future,
including actions and possible consequences.

Exercise 2: Work alone or with a partner. Write the correct letter on the line.

1. If the electricity goes off, __d__

2. If the answering machine isn't working, _____

3. If the remote control doesn't work, _____

4. If you can't get the CD out of the player, _____

5. If the computer freezes, _____

6. If your pager is stolen, _____

a. you'll have to reboot.

b. you won't get any messages.

c. you'll need to check the batteries.

d. you'll have to reset your alarm clock.

e. you'll have to buy a new one.

f. you'll have to get it repaired.

Your Turn

In your notebook write two sentences for another person to complete.
For the first sentence write an action with *if*. For the second sentence
write a possible consequence.

In Your Experience

Circle the names of the machines in Exercise 2. Put a check mark next
to each machine you have at home or work. Compare your circles and check
marks with a partner. Think about problems you've had with machines.
Write about them or tell your partner.

Person to Person

Listen to these conversations. With a partner finish the last conversation.
Use the conditional with *will* if you can. Then practice the conversations
with your partner.

CARLOS: What's taking you so long? If you don't
hurry, we'll be late.

OTILIA: I'm trying to set the VCR. I want to tape
60 Minutes.

CARLOS: So what's the problem?

OTILIA: There's no problem. I'll finish sooner
if you stop talking to me.

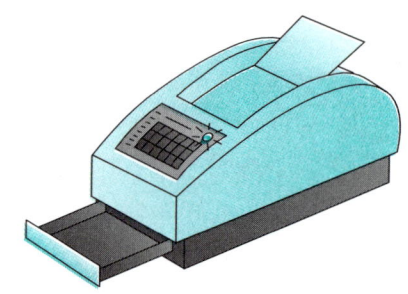

MARTIN: Did you receive the fax I sent?

JOEL: No, I didn't. I think you did something
wrong.

MARTIN: I'll try again. If I have another problem,
I'll call you back.

JOEL: OK.

CHRISTA: Mom, I can't get my bagel out of
the toaster.

LIZ: What do you mean?

CHRISTA: It's stuck, and it's starting to burn.

LIZ: Stop! Unplug the toaster! You'll get
a shock if you use a knife.

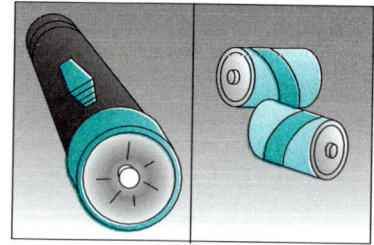

SAY: Where's the flashlight?

TAN: In the cabinet next to the stove.

SAY: Thanks. Oh no! It's not working.

TAN: _____

Your Turn

With a partner write a conversation about a frustrating problem with a machine.
Use the future conditional. Share your conversation with a group or the class.

VOCABULARY PROMPTS

In small groups talk about the meaning of these words.
Write a sentence for each one in your notebook.

security code   recipient   system   control   hear

READING FOR REAL

Jashoda works at a large company. The company just started using voice mail to
send and receive messages. Read the instructions below for using voice mail.

EZ-COM VOICE MAIL

TO GET INTO YOUR MAILBOX
Call system phone number (3000).
- Press 3.
- Enter your mailbox number (4169).
- Enter your security code (609).

TO RECORD A MESSAGE
- To record, press 4.
- To end recording press #.
- To send, press #.

TO LISTEN TO MESSAGES
- Press 3.
- To listen to last message, press 1–3.

USE THESE KEYS TO CONTROL YOUR MESSAGE
- To back up, press 5.
- To back up to beginning, press 5–5.
- To go forward, press 2.

TO SEND A QUICK MESSAGE
(Record a message without entering your mailbox.)
- Press *.
- Enter recipient's mailbox number.
- Record message and hang up.

Exercise 3: Answer these questions about the instructions.

1. These instructions tell how to
   a. use voice mail.
   b. buy voice mail.
   c. cancel voice mail.

2. If Jashoda wants to get into her mailbox, she'll press
   a. 3000-4169-609.
   b. 3000-#-4169-609.
   c. 3000-4169-609-#.

3. Jashoda is in her mailbox. If she wants to listen to messages, she'll press
   a. *.   b. 3.   c. 4.

4. Jashoda hears three messages. If she wants to listen to the first one again, she'll press
   a. 1–3.   b. 5–5.   c. #-#.

5. On another day Jashoda is in a hurry. She just wants to leave a message for Maria. She should press
   a. 4172*.   b. 4172.   c. *4172.

Talk About It

With a partner talk about the questions below.

What is voice mail? What are the advantages of having voice mail?
Can you think of any disadvantages?

CULTURE CORNER

In a small group talk about the meaning of the words on the time line.
If you need help, use a dictionary or ask your teacher.

SCIENCE AND TECHNOLOGY INVENTIONS (1807–1946)

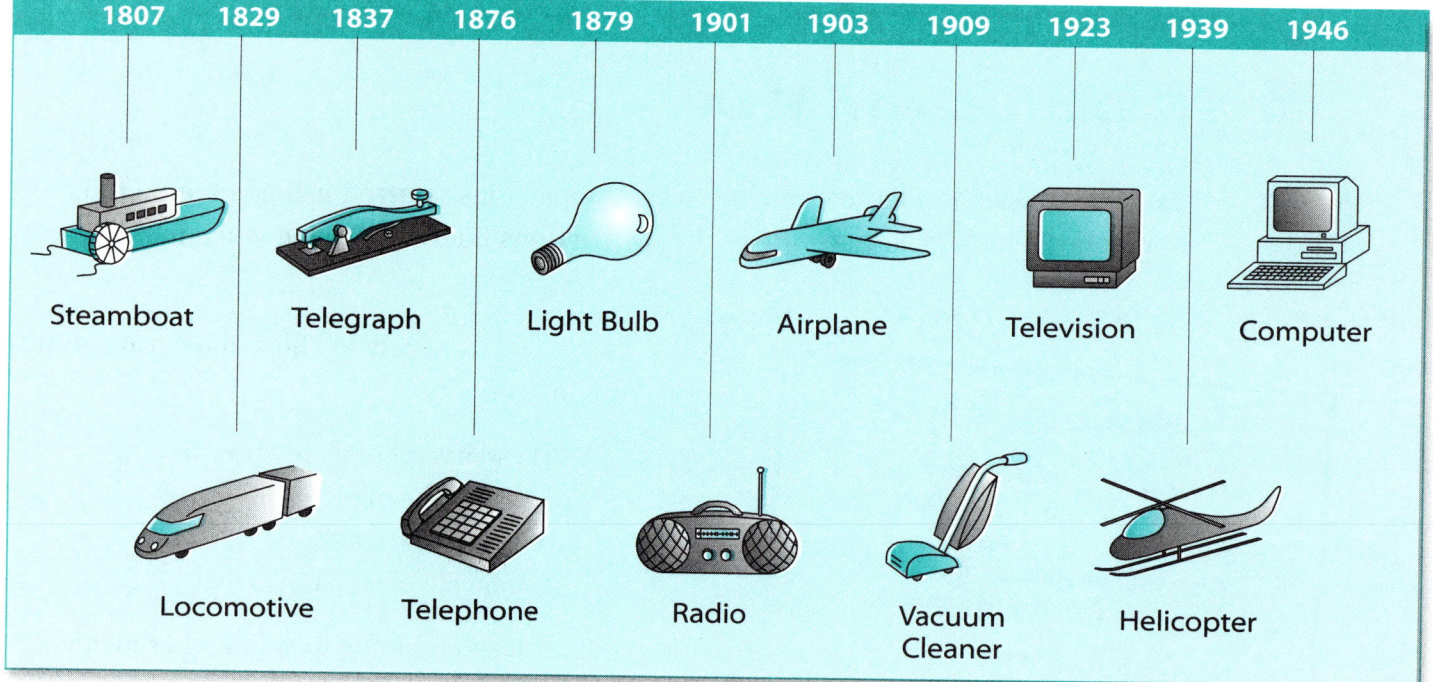

Exercise 4: Talk with a partner about the machines in the time line.
Which inventions do people really need and use? Which ones could
people live without?

Your Turn

In small groups make a list of inventions since 1946 in your notebook.
The group with the most inventions wins! (Hint: What are some appliances
or machines you use at home or work?)

In Your Experience

Draw your own technology time line. When did you get your first telephone?
car? camera? microwave? Share your answers with the class.

 Read the comic strip with a partner. Ask each other the questions below. Then share your answers with another pair or the class.

Roberto is at work talking to his friend Luis about his phone bill problems.

FACTS	Where are the men? What is Roberto showing Luis?
FEELINGS	How does Roberto feel? How does Luis feel?
AND YOU?	Have you ever had a problem like this? What happened?
COMPARISONS	Would parents in your country make their children pay for a phone bill?
ACTIONS	What can Roberto do to make sure this doesn't happen again?

 ## SOUND BITES

Roberto is talking to Luis about his phone bill.

Before You Listen In a small group talk about the ways you can try to lower your phone bills. Make a list.

While You Listen Look at your list of ways to lower phone bills. Put a check next to the ideas that are the same as Roberto's.

After You Listen Check your list with another group. Add new ideas to your list. Share your list with another group or the class.

SPOTLIGHT ON PHRASAL VERBS

He's **looking up** the number.   He's **picking up** the phone.

The meaning of phrasal verbs is usually different from the meaning
of each word alone. For more on phrasal verbs, see the Appendix.

Exercise 5: Choose phrasal verbs from the list to complete the sentences below.

| call back | hang up | look up | put on |
| call up | keep on | pick up | take off |

1. Can you _____ the phone? It's ringing.

2. I _____ trying, but the number is always busy.

3. Can you _____ a number for me?

4. I think I'll _____ an old friend tonight.

5. Can you _____? I'm really busy now.

6. I don't talk to salespeople. I just _____.

Person to Person

Listen to the conversations. Practice them with a partner.
Then change them to be true for you.

KIM: What's the matter?

LEE: I keep on getting a busy signal.

KIM: Why don't you call back later?

LEE: Good idea.

IAN: Mom, I really need a new computer.

MOM: So save up your money and buy one.

IAN: Can't you buy it for me? I'll pay
      you back.

MOM: Maybe you can pick one up on sale.

Your Turn

With a partner write a conversation with phrasal verbs.
Share the conversation with the class.

SPOTLIGHT ON SEPARABLE PHRASAL VERBS

Pay back the money.	**Pay** the money **back.**	**Pay** it **back.**
Pick up the groceries.	**Pick** the groceries **up.**	**Pick** them **up.**
Hang up the phone.	**Hang** the phone **up.**	**Hang** it **up.**
Call up George.	**Call** George **up.**	**Call** him **up.**
Look up the number.	**Look** the number **up.**	**Look** it **up.**

Many phrasal verbs are separable. A noun can come between the two parts. If you use a pronoun, it must come between the two parts. Other phrasal verbs are never separated. You must memorize which verbs are separable.

Exercise 6: Separate the phrasal verbs in each sentence below. Then write the sentence with a pronoun.

1. Pick up <u>the phone</u>.   Pick <u> the phone </u> up.   <u> Pick it up </u>.

2. Call up <u>Stacy</u>.   Call _____ up.   _____

3. Hang up <u>the phone</u>.   Hang _____ up.   _____

4. Look up <u>the names</u>.   _____   _____

5. Drop off <u>the letters</u>.   _____   _____

6. Turn down <u>the volume</u>.   _____   _____

In Your Experience

Write a short paragraph about yourself to share.
Use a separable phrasal verbs with and without pronouns.

GET GRAPHIC

Read the graph below.

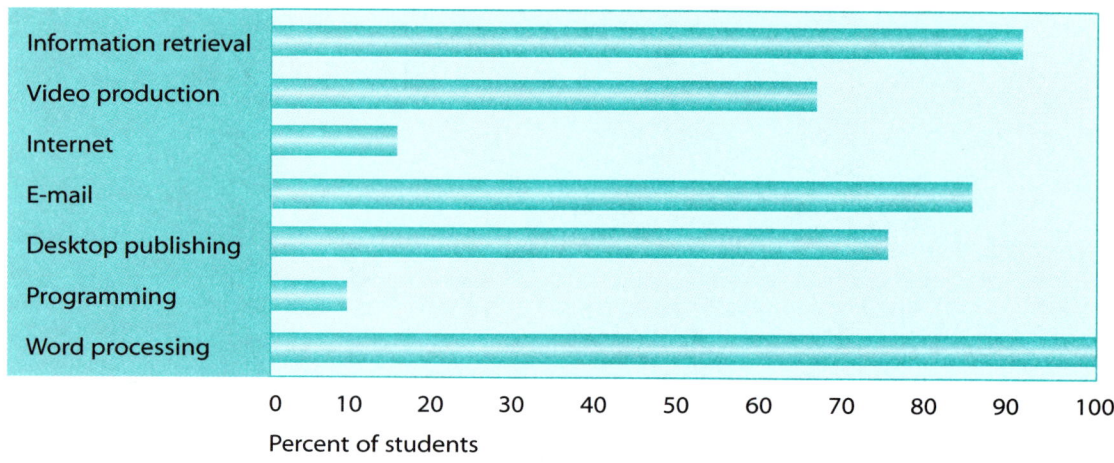

HOW STUDENTS USE COMPUTERS AT GLENAIR SCHOOL

Information retrieval
Video production
Internet
E-mail
Desktop publishing
Programming
Word processing

0   10   20   30   40   50   60   70   80   90   100

Percent of students

 Exercise 7: Match the technology in Column A with its use in Column B.

COLUMN A

1. Desktop publishing _____

2. E-mail _____

3. Information retrieval _____

4. Internet _____

5. Programming _____

6. Video production _____

7. Word processing _____

COLUMN B

a. finding a book in the library

b. writing a paper for school

c. using computer languages

d. making a commercial for cable TV

e. sending messages

f. searching for bargain software

g. designing a flyer

  Exercise 8: Use the information in the bar graph to complete the paragraph below.

Computers are most commonly used at the Glenair School for (1) _____

and (2) _____. Approximately (3) _____ percent of the students

use e-mail and (4) _____ percent use the Internet. Seventy-five percent

of the students use computers for (5) _____.

  In Your Experience

Is your class computer-literate? Do a survey. Ask questions such as the following.

How many people have used e-mail? How many have done word processing?
How many people have used the Internet? Use the answers to make a graph.

ISSUES AND ANSWERS

Read the letters below. If you don't know the meaning of a word, use a dictionary or ask your teacher. Write an answer to "Overworked."

Ask ABDUL and ANITA

DEAR ABDUL:

I have a problem. I have e-mail at work, and I have a very difficult boss. I e-mailed some bad things about her to a co-worker, and now I think my boss read the mail. She seems angry, and I'm afraid I'm going to get fired. Please help me.

WORRIED

DEAR WORRIED:

I am afraid you are right to be worried about being fired. E-mail is never private, even if you have a password. Never use e-mail for anything private or confidential. Another bit of advice: never say anything bad about the people you work with because they are sure to hear about it from someone!

ABDUL

DEAR ANITA:

I need help. I work in a factory. They installed a new computer system, and there have been a lot of layoffs. There are fewer people working, and now they want us to do twice as much work in half the time. If I complain, I'm afraid I'll get laid off. What should I do?

OVERWORKED

DEAR OVERWORKED:

_____

_____

_____

_____

_____

Exercise 9: Now write your own letter in your notebook asking for advice. Your partner will answer the letter.

Exercise 10: Present your letter and answer to the class.

WRAP-UP

With a group make an idea map about ways to save on telephone bills.
Use the conditional with *will* and phrasal verbs.

Present your ideas to another group or the class.

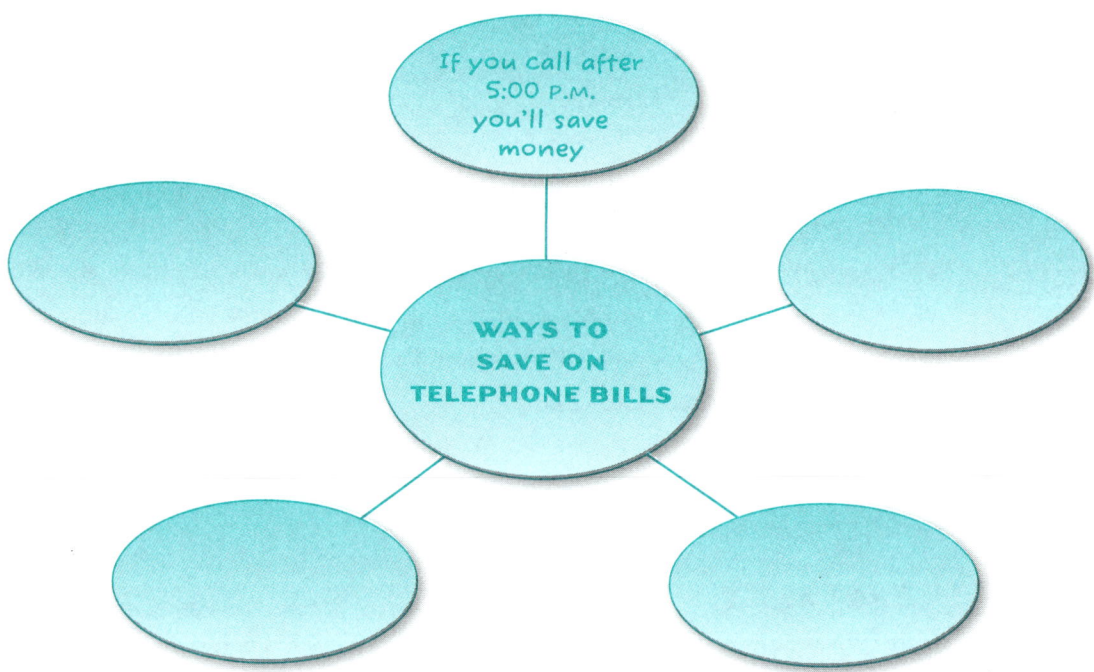

WAYS TO SAVE ON TELEPHONE BILLS

If you call after 5:00 P.M. you'll save money

Think About Learning

In this unit you learned a variety of skills and language structures.
Look at the items below and check how easy or difficult each one was for you.
At the bottom write one other thing you learned.

SKILLS / STRUCTURES	Page	easy ☺	so-so 😐	difficult ☹
Talk about people's problems	109, 115			
Understand recorded messages	110			
Understand conversations	112			
Read instructions for voice mail	113			
Make a technology time line	114			
Read a bar graph	118			
Read about and solve problems	119			
Use an idea map to present ideas	120			
Use the conditional with *will*	111			
Use phrasal verbs	116, 117			

APPENDIX

COMMON PRESENT AND PAST PARTICIPLES

Base Form	Simple Past	Present Participle	Past Participle
be	was, were	being	been
become	became	becoming	become
break	broke	breaking	broken
bring	brought	bringing	brought
buy	bought	buying	bought
catch	caught	catching	caught
come	came	coming	come
cut	cut	cutting	cut
do	did	doing	done
eat	ate	eating	eaten
fly	flew	flying	flown
give	gave	giving	given
go	went	went	gone
have	had	having	had
hold	held	holding	held
keep	kept	keeping	kept
know	knew	knew	known
leave	left	leaving	left
make	made	making	made
meet	met	meeting	met
put	put	putting	put
read	read	reading	read
ride	rode	riding	ridden
run	ran	running	run
say	said	saying	said
see	saw	seeing	seen
send	sent	sending	sent
sit	sat	sitting	sat
speak	spoke	speaking	spoken
take	took	taking	taken
teach	taught	teaching	taught
tell	told	telling	told
think	thought	thinking	thought
understand	understood	understanding	understood
write	wrote	writing	written

ADVERBS OF TIME

The manager seemed very friendly **while** he was talking on the phone.

We were feeling very positive **until** we met him.

When the time clause comes first, use a comma.
Before we met the manager, we were excited about the apartment.

As soon as we walked into the office, things changed.

When we walked into his office, he didn't seem friendly anymore.

ADVERBS OF OPPOSITION

Some people are for handguns, **while** other people are against them.

Although handguns can help you protect yourself, they can also be used to kill innocent people.

Some states have strict gun laws, **whereas** other states don't.

You can also use *though* and *even though* as adverbs of opposition.

COMMON PHRASAL VERBS

Verbs	Meaning
(I) = the verb cannot be separated	
call (someone) back	to return someone's call
call (someone) up	to call someone
clean (something) out	to clean the inside of something
get back (I)	to return home
grow up (I)	to become an adult
hang (something) up	to return the receiver to the telephone
hold on (I)	to wait
keep on (I)	to continue to do something
look (something) up	to look for something in a book
pick(something) out	to choose
pick (something) up	to lift something
put (something) on	to dress in
speak up (I)	to speak louder
take (something) off	to remove (clothing)
throw (something) away	to put something in the trash